Grain
for the
Famine

James Jacob Prasch

First published in Australia 1999

MORIEL – GOD IS MY TEACHER

MORIEL MINISTRIES AUSTRALIA
P. O. Box 7017
Noble Park East, Victoria, 3174
Telephone: +61 3 9774 8523
Email: moriel@satlink.com.au
Website: www.moriel.org

This Edition published in the UK 2000
St Matthew Publishing Ltd
24 Geldart St.
Cambridge CB1 2LX
+ (0)1223 504871
fax + (0)1223 512304
Email: PF.SMP@dial.pipex.com

ISBN 19015460 8 X

Contents:

FOREWORD

I WAS introduced to Jacob Prasch through mutual friends Barry and Andrew Smith. At the time I was writing for Barry's *Omega Times* Christian newspaper. Andrew asked me to review some video tapes of a "new evangelist to the Jews" they had met in their ministry travels in UK. I was enthralled as I listened to fresh insights on old Scriptural themes, which the speaker referred to as "Biblical Midrash." There was his *Abraham's Journey—A Journey Like Ours; The Autumn Feasts; Jewish-Arab Reconciliation in Christ;* and others. Shortly after I completed my assignment, the speaker accompanied Barry Smith on a ministry tour of New Zealand, when I met him at a large public meeting held in Victory Chapel, Auckland. So commenced a friendship, which has lasted for some six or so years.

Jacob Prasch and I have shared platforms in New Zealand, Australia and in Great Britain where we have each helped to organise meetings for the other. We have travelled many thousands of miles together by car and by plane, being accommodated in the same homes and have developed a mutual respect for each other. The things that most impress me about Jacob is his unwavering courage to stand against heresy and to oppose error in the face of great opposition and his strong commitment to truth. Those who know him are well aware of his readiness to face controversy head on.

He has his critics, sometimes based on misunderstandings and at others on disagreements. Some have criticised his system of hermeneutics based on what he calls *"midrash"* equating it with the extra-biblical *"midrashim"* of the Jewish tradition. In this I am convinced that his critics are wrong. Jacob speaks out strongly against the false Hebrew Roots Movements of our time and has always distanced himself from anything that savours of non-biblicism. His emphasis is very similar to that of the Open Brethren and early Pentecostal preachers who derived much spiritual truth from what we generally refer to as typology. In fact there are a number of parallels between *"midrash"* as viewed and taught by Jacob Prasch and typological preaching that has been my own pattern and pursuit throughout 40 plus years of ministry.

There are additional elements in Mr Prasch's system, which will become clear to the studious as you read the following twelve chapters all of which were given as sermons, in the first instance and should be read with that in mind.

In these days when there is undoubtedly a famine of the Word of God as popular preachers tell stories, frequently about themselves, rather than expound the Scriptures, we should be thrilled when someone with Mr Prasch's background, training and scholarship presents such thoroughly biblical teaching.

I pray that this and other of his writings will have a wide readership and that the truth contained in the messages will bless you as much as those early video tapes blessed me.

PHILIP L. POWELL

Philip L. Powell

Christian Witness Ministries PO Box 341
Healesville Victoria
3777 Australia

Email: philip@christian-witness.org
or *maureen@christian-witness-org*
Web site: http://www.christian-witness.org

MIDRASH

IF you look at the way the New Testament quotes the Old Testament, it is clear that the apostles did not use western protestant methods of exegesis or interpretation. Jesus was a rabbi. Paul was a rabbi. They interpreted the bible in the way other rabbis did—according to a method called *midrash*.

Something went wrong in the early church; it got away from its Jewish roots. And as more Gentiles became Christians, something that Paul warned (in Romans 11) should not happen, happened. People lost sight of the root.

Whenever there is a change in world-view, there is going to be a change in theology. A positive way to handle that change is called 'recontextualising'; a negative way is called 'redefining'. When the Wycliffe Bible Translators translated Isaiah 1:18, *Though your sins are like scarlet, they shall be white as snow,* for tribal people in equatorial Africa—a place where the people had never seen snow—they translated it as "they shall be white as coconut." That is recontextualising—taking the same truth and putting it into the context of somebody else's language or culture or world-view. That is perfectly valid; it does no harm to the message, in contrast to *redefinition*. Instead of re-explaining what the bible means, redefinition *changes* what the bible means. That is wrong. And that is what happened in the early church.

After Constantine the Great turned Christianity into the religion of the state, people began redefining the gospel in increasingly radical ways. Some of the early church fathers believed that what was best in Greek theosophy, for example the monotheistic ideas of Plato and Socrates, helped to prepare the Greek world for the coming of Jesus, in the same way that the Torah (the Old Testament) prepared the Jewish world.

Up to a point, that is a fair statement. There is a Greek (Hellenistic) way of thinking and there is a Hebrew (Hebraic) way of thinking. Paul used both. When Paul spoke to the Jews he used the Hebrew way of thinking, but in Athens when he was preaching the gospel to the Areopagites (Acts 1 7:22-31), he used the Greek way of thinking. Jews seek a sign, Greeks seek wisdom. There is validity in both, if they are used biblically.

A problem arose when people began to Heilenise a Jewish faith. Instead of recontextualising the gospel for Greeks, they began redefining it in Greek terms. This happened especially in Alexandria in the time of Origen, but it became a major problem after Constantine, with the introduction of the teachings of Augustine of Hippo, and the people who influenced him—Cyprian of Carthage, Ambrose, and others. The Greeks knew many things from Plato and Socrates that were true, such as the fact that man is made in God's image and likeness. Even people with no Judeo-Christian background and no access to the bible can know by natural reason there is one true God and that man is sinful (Romans 1:18-20).

We can agree with the things in Greek theosophy up to the point they agree with the bible, but when people begin reinterpreting and redefining the gospel in the light of a Greek world-view, we have a problem.

The Greeks believed in dualism. They thought that everything of the flesh was bad and everything of the spirit was good.

A Greek reading the words: *In the beginning was the Word, and the Word was with God, and the Word was God* (John 1:1), could agree with them. But he could not agree with the statement: *The Word became flesh* (John 1:14).

The Greeks believed that something physical was bad, simply because it was physical.

The bible teaches that the spiritual and the physical were meant to work in harmony with each other. There was not to be any contradiction or any conflict between the two. The flesh is fallen, that is true, but there is nothing wrong with the physical elements themselves.

Augustine did not recontextualise but, rather, redefined Christianity as a Greek, Platonic religion. He said things like, "The only good thing about marriage is having children who will be celibate". These ideas were introduced into the Greek world by the Manichaeans, who said that the first sin was having marital relations. That is why, to this day, Roman Catholicism cannot handle sexuality, and why it has so many hangups, and why Roman Catholics are even hungup about marital sex.

Midrash uses typology and allegory—symbols—in order to illustrate and illumine doctrine. For instance, Jesus is "the Passover Lamb." The symbolism of the Jewish Passover perfectly illustrates the doctrine of atonement, but we never base the doctrine of atonement on the symbolism. The symbolism illustrates the doctrine, which is itself stated plainly elsewhere in scripture.

In the gnostic world of Greek thinking, the opposite happens. Gnostics claim to have received a subjective, mystical insight—called a *gnosis*— into the symbols. They then re-interpret the plain meaning of the text in light of the *gnosis*. For gnostics, symbolism is the basis for their doctrine, contrary to the ancient Jewish methods.

Gnostic methods started to creep into the church through people who were influenced by Philo. His teachings progressively entered Roman Catholicism to the point where Augustine could say, "If God used violence to convert Paul, the church can use violence to convert people," which led to the crusades, the Spanish Inquisition and so on. Instead of recontextualising, they were redefining scripture. They were reading a Jewish book as if it were a Greek book. That was a mistake. It started with Origen in the east and Augustine in the west, and steadily worsened over the centuries. It became much worse in the Middle Ages with something called *Scholasticism*. Judaism was rewritten as an Aristotelian religion by Moses Maimonides, then Christianity was rewritten as an Aristotelian religion by Thomas Aquinas. The reformers came along and tried to correct what had gone wrong in medieval Roman Catholicism.

Unfortunately, although the reformers were dynamic personalities, they were not dynamic thinkers. The reformation was born out of something called *Humanism*. [Note: the first humanists were not secular, they were Christians.] The best of the humanists were men like Thomas à Kempis, John Colet, and Jacques Lefèvre. But the greatest of them all was Erasmus of Rotterdam. Luther, Calvin, Zwingli and most of the other reformers got their ideas from Erasmus.

Erasmus and the other humanists attempted to study and teach the bible in its plain literal meaning, in order to undo the medieval abuses of Roman Catholicism. They placed the emphasis on reading the bible as literature and as history, and gave us the system of grammatical-historical exegesis that has been used in the protestant churches ever since.

The problem with the reformers is that they only went so far. They made rules governing the application of their grammatical-historical system in order to refute medieval Roman Catholicism, and many of those rules are still taught in theological seminaries today. One such rule is this: *There are many applications of a scripture but only one interpretation.* That is total rubbish! The Talmud tells us there are multiple interpretations. Who did Jesus agree with? The reformers? Or the other rabbis?

Jesus said, *A wicked and adulterous generation asks for a miraculous sign! But none will be given it except the sign of the prophet Jonah* (Matthew 12:39). What was "the sign of the prophet Jonah"? In one place Jesus said it was that "*as Jonah was three days and nights in the stomach of a huge fish, so the Son of Man will be three days and three nights in the heart of the earth*" (Matthew 12:40). But, at the same time, He said that it was the fact that the men of Nineveh repented at the preaching of Jonah (Luke 11:32). The Gentiles would repent when the Jews did not: that is also the sign of the prophet Jonah. He gave two equally valid interpretations of what that sign is.

So, where protestant hermeneutics say that there is only one interpretation, all the rest is application – it is out of step with Jesus.

Another rule of reformed hermeneutics says that, *if the plain wording of Scripture makes sense, seek no other sense.* Take it at its face value, full stop. That is also total rubbish!

A first or second century Jewish Christian reading John's gospel, chapters one, two and three, would have said it was the story of the new creation, a midrash on *Bereshith* (Genesis) chapters one, two and three—the story of the creation. He would have seen that God walked the earth in Genesis, and now God walked the earth again in the new creation in John. He would have seen that the Spirit moved on the water and brought forth the creation in Genesis, and now the Spirit moved on the water and brought forth the new creation in John. He would have seen that God came and separated light from dark in the creation in Genesis, and now He separated the light from dark in the new creation in John. He would have seen that there was the small light and the great light in the creation in Genesis, and now there was the small light—John the Baptist—and the great light—Jesus—in the new creation in John.

The fig tree, midrashically, in Jewish metaphor, represents the Tree of Life that we see in the garden in Genesis, in Ezekiel 47, and in the Book of Revelation. So when Jesus told Nathaniel, *"I saw you while you were still under the fig tree"* (John 1:48), He was not simply saying to Nathaniel that He saw him under a literal fig tree (although He did), He was telling him that He had seen him from the garden, from the creation, from the foundation of the world.

By reading the bible as literature and history, as the humanists did, you only see part of it.

The humanists were reacting to medieval scholasticism and the gnosticism that much of Roman Catholicism is based upon. Nonetheless, their approach prevents people from seeing much of the depth of scripture. Using the grammatical-historical method, the reformers were able to discover truths such as justification by faith and the authority of scripture. But that is all they could see; they could not go beyond it.

Martin Luther considered Romans to be the main book of the bible. He totally rejected the Book of Revelation. Yet the Book of Revelation is the book for the last days. Luther admitted that you cannot understand it with a protestant mind. What is wrong? Is the Book of Revelation wrong? Or is the protestant mind wrong? The protestant mind is wrong. God put Revelation in the bible. It means *apokalypsis* (Gk.), an unveiling, and it will be unveiled.

Be very careful. Daniel (Daniel 12:4) and John (Revelation 10:4) were told to "seal these things up" until the time of the end. In the fullness of God's time, the interpretation of these books will be manifested to the faithful. When you see people writing out diagrams and charts, saying that they have got the whole eschatological program and all of Revelation figured out, be very cautious. It is sealed up until the appropriate time. God will unveil it in His way and in His time. And that will be done step by step. The first step is going back to reading the bible as a Jewish book, instead of as a Greek one.

The epistles are commentary on other scripture; they tell you what other scripture means on a very practical level. It is fine to read the epistles as literature and history, using grammatical-historical methods. But there are different kinds of literature in the bible, different literary *genres* that God put in there for different reasons. Psalms—Hebrew poetry; Revelation—apocalyptic literature; the gospels—narrative; Proverbs—wisdom literature.

You do not read a letter in the same way as you read poetry. You do not read *The Chronicles of Narnia* (C.S.Lewis) in the same way as you would read a letter from Aunt Harriet back in England.

If you read the epistles, you will see that the apostles did not interpret the other books of the bible by the grammatical-historical method. The book of Hebrews is a commentary on the symbolism of the Levitical priesthood and the temple. Look at Galatians 4:24 onwards, the story of the two women - it is a midrash on the purpose of the Law.

Look at the epistle of Jude. It is midrashic literature (and we will examine it in the next chapter).

The apostles did not handle the scriptures according to protestant grammatical-historical methods.

There are different kinds of prophecy in the bible. The two kinds that are important in understanding the last days are messianic prophecies and, connected to those, eschatological prophecies. When we come to consider biblical prophecy, this is very important, because the western mind, with its basis in sixteenth century humanism, says that prophecy consists of a prediction and a fulfilment.

To the ancient Jewish mind, it was not a question of something being predicted, then being fulfilled. That is a wrong view of biblical prophecy. Rather, prophecy was a *pattern* which is recapitulated; a prophecy having multiple fulfilments. And each cycle teaches something about the ultimate fulfilment.

For example: in a famine, Abraham went into Egypt (Genesis 12:10-20). God judged Pharaoh. Abraham and his descendants came out of Egypt, taking the wealth of Egypt with them, and went into the Promised Land. Abraham's descendants replayed the same experience. In a famine they went into Egypt (Genesis 42). Again, God judged the wicked king, Pharaoh. Abraham's descendants came out of Egypt, taking the wealth of Egypt with them (Exodus 12:36), and they went into the Promised Land. What happened to Abraham happened to his descendants.

Then the same thing happened with Jesus. *When they had gone, an angel of the Lord appeared to Joseph in a dream. "Get up," he said "take the child and his mother and escape to Egypt. Stay there until I tell you, for Herod is going to search for the child to kill him." So he got up, took the child and his mother during the night and left for Egypt, where he stayed until the death of Herod. And so was fulfilled what the Lord had said through the prophet: "Out of Egypt I called my son"* (Matthew 2:16).

Matthew says that when Jesus came out of Egypt, after King Herod died, that fulfilled the prophecy of Hosea. *"When Israel was a child, I loved him, and out of Egypt I called my son."* (Hosea 11:1-2). Very plainly, Hosea chapter 11 is talking about the Exodus, about what happened with Moses. In its grammatical-historical context, it is talking about the Exodus, not about the Messiah. But Matthew appears to take the passage out of all reasonable context and twist it into talking about Jesus. We have to ask, is Matthew wrong? Or is there something wrong with our protestant way of interpreting the bible?

There is nothing wrong with Matthew, and there is nothing wrong with the New Testament. But there is something wrong with our protestant mentality. The Jewish idea of prophecy is not prediction, but *pattern.*

Abraham came out of Egypt when Pharaoh was judged; his descendants' came out of Egypt when the wicked king was judged; then another wicked king was judged and the Messiah came out of Egypt. There are multiple fulfilments of prophecy. Midrashically, "Israel" alludes to *Yeshua* (Jesus) the Messiah. When you see verses like: *Israel my glory and Israel my first born,* they are midrashic allusions to the Messiah.

Then, in 1 Corinthians 10, something else happens: We come out of Egypt, which Paul tells us is a symbol of the world. Pharaoh, who was deified by the Egyptians and worshipped as God, is a symbol of the devil, the god of this world. Just as Moses made a covenant with blood and sprinkled it on the people, so did Jesus. Moses fasted forty days, and so did Jesus. Jesus is the prophet like Moses, predicted in Deuteronomy 18:18. Just as Moses led the children of Israel out of Egypt, through the water, into the Promised Land, so Jesus leads us out of the world, through baptism, into heaven. It is a pattern. Then *the horse and its rider are thrown into the sea* (Exodus 15:1). We sing the song of Moses—*the horse and rider thrown into the sea*—in Revelation 15:3. Why? Because it is a pattern. The ultimate meaning of "coming out of Egypt" is the resurrection and rapture of the church.

The judgements that happen in Exodus are replayed in Revelation. And just as Pharaoh's magicians were able to counterfeit the miracles of Moses and Aaron, so the Antichrist and False Prophet will counterfeit the miracles of Jesus and His witnesses. They brought Joseph's bones with them when they came out of Egypt (Exodus 13:19). Why? Because it is a pattern. The dead in Christ will rise first.

The ancient Jewish mind that produced the New Testament looks at prophecy, not as prediction, but as pattern. To understand what is going to happen in the future, you look at what did happen in the past. There are multiple fulfilments, and each successive fulfilment teaches something about the ultimate fulfilment.

You will never understand the Book of Revelation with the limited approach to biblical interpretation that is taught in protestant seminaries. Midrash is like a quadratic equation or a very complex second order differential equation, a thirteen or fourteen step equation. Some people take the first step of grammatical-historical exegesis and think the equation is solved. There is nothing wrong with what they do, but there is plenty wrong with what they do not do. The equation is not solved. There is nothing wrong with grammatical-historical exegesis. It is a necessary first step, it is a necessary preliminary, and it is okay for reading the epistles. But that is all.

It takes the wisdom of the ancients to really understand these things *Let him that hath understanding count the number of the beast...* (Revelation 13:18)—not the wisdom of the 16th century, but the wisdom of the first century.

BACKSLIDERS IN THE CHURCH

THE epistle of Jude contains the warnings of history to the ungodly. Jude is often considered to be the brother of Jesus, but there are debates about the question.

Nonetheless we know that the early church held the book of Jude to be canonical. One of the things Jude wrote against was *incipient gnosticism,* referring to the beginnings of gnostic influences that were then creeping into the church.

There are two things about Jude that are extraordinary. The first is that it is the most classic example of midrash in the New Testament. The second is its subject matter (part of which is also found in Peter's epistle), that is, the subject of false believers who remain within the church. There are probably as many backsliders in the church as there are those who have left.

The definition of a "backslider" is not someone who has left the church. Leaving the church is the result of being a backslider. Rather a backslider is someone who has forsaken their relationship with Jesus. But the flesh loves religion, and people have a natural tendency to mask their true spiritual state. And that is what Jude's epistle deals with: people who are backslidden, but who camouflage their real state with their religion.

Jude, a bond-servant of Jesus Christ, and brother of James, to those who are the called, beloved in God the Father, and kept for Jesus Christ: May mercy and peace and love be multiplied to you. Beloved, while I was making every effort to write to you about our common salvation, I felt the necessity to write to you appealing that you contend earnestly for the faith which was once for all delivered to the saints. For certain persons have crept in unnoticed, those who were long beforehand marked out for this condemnation, ungodly persons who turn the grace of our God into licentiousness and deny our only Master and Lord, Jesus Christ (Jude 1-4).

Certain persons have crept in unnoticed, and he says they are people who deny our Lord Jesus Christ, and who turn the grace of God into licentiousness. He is probably alluding to certain gnostic beliefs about who Jesus was and what He was. But obviously these people did not deny Jesus in the sense of saying "I don't believe in Him." These were people who denied Him in terms of their doctrine and their lives.

One way in which they did this was licentiousness. Legalism is one thing, antinomianism is just the opposite. *Antinomianism* means 'without law.' The word refers to people who say, "I am free in Christ, I can do what I want," and then proceed to live immoral lives. The New Testament says the opposite is true. *Unless your righteousness surpasses that of the scribes and Pharisees, you shall not enter the kingdom of heaven* (Matthew 5:20). By any kind of religious or legalistic standard, the Pharisees were very righteous, but that is nothing like the life of being born again.

Now I desire to remind you, though you know all things once for all, that the Lord, after saving a people out of the land of Egypt, subsequently destroyed those who did not believe (Jude 5).

This is the same language Paul used in 1 Corinthians 10—they came out of Egypt with us, but they did not believe. There will be people in the fellowship who will not be part of the fellowship.

And angels who did not keep their own domain, but abandoned their proper abode, He has kept in eternal bonds under darkness for the judgment of the great day

(Jude 6). This speaks of the nephilim (Genesis 6:4).

Just as Sodom and Gomorrah and the cities around them, since they in the same way as these indulged in gross immorality and went after strange flesh [homosexuality], *are exhibited as an example, in undergoing the punishment of eternal fire* (Jude 7). We do not normally think of anybody who comes to church as being as bad as the violent Sodomite gangs of Sodom and Gomorrah, but let us notice how God thinks.

Yet in the same manner these men, also by dreaming, defile the flesh, and reject authority, and revile angelic majesties.

But Michael the archangel, when he disputed with the devil and argued about the body of Moses, did not dare pronounce against him a railing judgment, but said, "The Lord rebuke you".

But these men revile the things which they do not understand; and the things which they know by instinct, like unreasoning animals, by these things they are destroyed (Jude 8-10).

One of the versions of this heresy in the early church were people who said, "I am a new creation. I have an old creation and a new creation. It doesn't matter what the old creation does, it is not going to heaven. It is the new creation that is going to go heaven, so I can go out and do what I want!" I have met Christians who, even though they would not put it in those terms, live lives that say the same thing.

Woe to them! For they have gone the way of Cain, and for pay they have rushed headlong into the error of Balaam, and perished in the rebellion of Korah (Jude 11) - as occurred in the wilderness. Now he begins a midrashic exposition.

These men are those who are hidden reefs in your love feasts when they feast with you without fear, caring for themselves... (Jude 12).

First Corinthians talks about those who partake of the Lord's supper in an unworthy manner. The early Christians followed the Jewish practice of a fellowship meal called an *agape*, from the Greek word for unconditional love—that is when and how they took the Lord's supper. It was the centrepiece of their worship and fellowship.

When people who are not walking with Jesus take the Lord's supper with you and your church, they are doing so without fear, and they are eating judgment unto themselves.

Now in no way do I want to suggest that I have anything good to say about Roman Catholicism, but I will tell you this: their view of the eucharist and communion is much higher than that of many Christians. They understand the seriousness of it to a degree far greater than many evangelicals.

The Plymouth Brethren have a very high and very biblical view of the Lord's supper. They will not let people take the Lord's supper who are not baptised. If they know someone has immorality in their life, they will not allow them to take the Lord's supper, and we should not either!

They are ... *clouds without water, carried along by winds...* (Jude 12).

We read in Hebrews 12:1 that we are surrounded by a *cloud of witnesses...* In scripture water speaks of the Holy Spirit. These people are clouds. In some sense they are witnesses, but the Holy Spirit is not in their witness. The Holy Spirit's presence and power is not in their testimony; living water does not flow from them. They may be witnesses, in the sense that they believe that Jesus died. They may even have experienced His salvation at some point, or at least professed faith in Him, but they are clouds without water. They are carried along by different winds. *Winds* in scripture speak of spirits (both *ruach* in Hebrew, and *pneuma* in Greek mean both "spirit" and "wind").

Autumn trees without fruit, doubly dead, uprooted (Jude 12).

Remember in Revelation when the fig tree is shaken and the fruit all falls off, and the sky is rolled up (Revelation 6:13-14)? Twice dead, doubly dead! They are alive, then they are dead again; trees without fruit who are uprooted. We have to understand about trees. We shall be called trees of righteousness (Isaiah 61:3). *The trees of the field will clap their hands* (Isaiah 55:12). The *Tree of Life* was in the garden (Genesis 2:9). It appears in Ezekiel 47:12, and it appears again in Revelation 22:14.

The *Tree of Life* in the garden has to do with Jesus. His nature was the fruit. If Adam and Eve had eaten of that fruit, they would have lived for ever. Adam and Eve were like this: they had no imperfections, but they were not yet perfected. Sort of like a little baby, a healthy, beautiful little baby. There is nothing wrong with the child, there is no imperfection, but not until it grows up will it be perfected.

That is the way Adam and Eve were—they were created without imperfection, but they were not yet perfected. They had a choice: to eat of the *Tree of Life,* or the *Tree of Knowledge of Good and Evil* under the deception of Satan; they made the wrong choice.

In the Middle East the leaves are necessary to protect the fruit. If there are no leaves, the fruit will be destroyed because the sun in the Middle East is so hot. The leaves are good, but they are not good enough. When Adam and Eve sinned, they tried to hide their nakedness by sewing fig leaves together. "Nakedness" in the bible does not mean physical nudity, it means not having the *garments of salvation* (Isaiah 61:10) or *robes washed... in the blood of the Lamb* (Revelation 7:14).

The leaves of the fig tree represent good works. That is why we read in Revelation 22:2, *the leaves of the tree were for the healing of the nations.* Good works have their value. Without the leaves the fruit is destroyed. In other words, as James puts it, *faith without works is dead* (James 2:17).

If there are no leaves your fruit will be destroyed. Your works are the evidence of your faith. My works are the evidence of my faith. On the other hand, you cannot eat leaves, you can only eat the fruit. So Jesus cursed the fig tree because it had leaves but no fruit (Matthew 21:19). Israel had a works' righteousness, but they did not have the fruit of the Spirit. Galatians 5:22—the fruit of the Spirit is love. 1 Corinthians 13:2—*If I do not have love, I am nothing.* You can have all manner of good works, but they amount to nothing.

These people are trees without fruit. Jesus cursed the fig tree. They are guilty of the same thing—they may have leaves, but they have no fruit. When Jesus cursed that fig tree it was not yet the season for figs. *The son of man is coming at an hour when you do not think He will* (Matthew 24:44).

They are wild waves of the sea, casting up their own shame like foam... (Jude 13).

We read about this in the Psalms. The figure of the sea has to do with the nations of the world. *Why are the nations in an uproar, and the peoples devising a vain thing? The kings of the earth take their stand, and the rulers take counsel together against the Lord and against His Anointed* (Psalm 2:1-2).

They are wandering stars, for whom the black darkness has been reserved forever (Jude 13).

God told Abraham that his descendants would be like the stars of heaven (Genesis 15:5). Stars are figures of spirits or angels in certain contexts. But they are also figures of believers, who have light in themselves (Matthew 5:14). These are figures of Christians—*wandering stars*—Christians who are not in a fixed orbit, who are doing their own thing.

And about these also Enoch [that is an Apocryphal book], *in the seventh generation from Adam, prophesied, saying, "Behold, the Lord came with many thousands of His holy ones, to execute judgment upon all and to convict all the ungodly of all their ungodly deeds which they have done in an ungodly way, and of all the harsh things which ungodly sinners have spoken against Him* (Jude 14–15).

He comes with His holy ones to execute this judgement. Restorationists say that is happening now. They claim the 'holy ones' are 'Joel's army' and they will bring this judgement before Jesus comes. But scripture says that the final judgement will happen when Jesus returns. When Restorationists pray, "Thy kingdom come," what they mean is "Thy kingdom HAS come." It is their movement; it is Kingdom Now. This teaching is just as wrong, at one extreme, as a bunker mentality is at the other. The kingdom is now, but not yet. Then Jude goes on to describe their behaviour.

These are grumblers, finding fault, following after their own lusts; they speak arrogantly, flattering people for the sake of gaining an advantage (Jude 16).

They flatter people for the sake of gaining a personal advantage. That is a sure sign of somebody who has a spiritual problem in the church they flatter people for the sake of personal gain. They are not seeking to encourage somebody—"God bless you sister, that was good; God bless you brother, that was good." It is the mentality of the world to flatter people in order to obtain certain positions.

But you, beloved, ought to remember the words that were spoken beforehand by the apostles of our Lord Jesus Christ [now notice this] *that they were saying to you, "In the last time there shall be mockers, following after their own ungodly lusts"* (Jude 17).

In the last days... These kinds of people have been around since the early church, but the main focus of Jude's emphasis is that in the last days they will multiply. The point is this, things that are true at any time in history become especially true in the last days. Jesus warned that there will be false teachers and false prophets coming among you. There have always been false teachers and false prophets coming to deceive God's people, but in the last days they multiply.

Midrash describes this as the principle of *kalveh homer*. It is a principle which St Paul studied in the school of Hillel. Literally translated as "light to heavy," it means that something that is true in a *light* situation becomes especially true in a *heavy* situation. In another example, Hebrews 10:25 urges us *not to forsake our own assembling together, as is the habit of some, but encouraging one another; and all the more, as you see the day drawing near.* Meeting together is always important, but in the last days it becomes especially important. Things that are always true become especially true in the last days. Things that are generally important become especially important as we get closer to the return of Jesus.

These are the ones who cause divisions. They are worldly minded, and devoid of the spirit. But you, beloved, building yourselves up on your most holy faith; praying in the Holy Spirit (Jude 19-20).

Some people take this expression 'praying in the Holy Spirit' to mean praying in tongues. It does not. If the Holy Spirit is in any particular prayer, that is 'praying in the Holy Spirit'. There are tongues of angels, and of men, but any prayer inspired by the Holy Spirit is praying in the Spirit.

Any prayer not inspired by the Holy Spirit is praying in the flesh. And I do believe in praying in tongues.

Keep yourselves in the love of God, waiting anxiously for the mercy of our Lord Jesus Christ to eternal life. And having mercy on some, who are doubting; save others, snatching them out of the fire (Jude 21-23).

We have many people today, particularly the people who organise the 'March for Jesus' in the UK, that are telling the unsaved that there is no such place as hell! That is the belief of Graham Kendrick, who writes the hymns, and of Roger Forster.

These people are our brethren in Christ. I am not saying they are not Christians. I am not judging them. I am simply saying they are telling unsaved people there is no eternal damnation. That is what is at the back of the 'March for Jesus'. They say, "If you don't repent and accept Jesus, after you die, you're not going to exist any more". Well, that is what unsaved people believe anyway, that there is a judgement, but then they are annihilated. You cannot prove from the bible that there is no such place as hell.

Have mercy on some who are doubting; save others, snatching them out of the fire; and on some have mercy with fear, hating even the garment polluted by the flesh (Jude 22-23).

Now it is not talking about a literal garment, it is talking midrashically about the garments of salvation, our white robes (Revelation 7:14).

Now to Him who is able to keep you from stumbling, and to make you stand in the presence of His glory blameless with great joy, to the only God our Saviour, through Jesus Christ our Lord, be glory, majesty, dominion, and authority, before all time and now and forever Amen (Jude 24-25).

This entire epistle, one chapter, can all be summed up in one verse from the Old Testament: *The backslider in heart will have his fill of his own ways, but a good man will be satisfied with his* (Proverbs 14:14).

Malcontents! If our basic needs are being met—spiritually, financially—it says in Timothy, we should be content.

If God adds to that, praise the Lord, that is His blessing and His goodness. Be a faithful steward of whatever He gives, but be content.

There are as many backsliders inside the church as there are outside. There are people in the church who have not turned their backs on the world, but they are trying to live in two creations, in two natures. They are trying to serve two masters. That tension, that struggle, that battle, rages in each and every one of us, every hour of every day.

There is an old man and a new man, an old woman and a new woman, an old creation and a new creation. The conflict between the two rages in all of us. The voice we hear, just by choosing to listen to it, determines who is going to win the fight.

There are as many backsliders in the church as the ones who have left, and I would venture—without any word of knowledge—there are probably among those reading this now those who are backslidden. How are they backslidden? *The backslider in heart will have his fill of his own ways*. That is the key.

God is warning us about people in the church—and if you are one of them, God is warning you about yourself. In the last days, people who are like this will eventually fall away. They can live their whole lives under deception, but in times of persecution these kinds of people are the ones who fall away.

And brother will deliver up brother to death... (Matthew 10:21).

It is going to be these kinds of people who will betray us, the ones who are filled with their own ways.

I ask one thing of the Lord, somehow, no matter what He has to do in my life, do not let me become one of them.

KASHRUT AND FAMINE

T HE Hebrew dietary laws are found in Deuteronomy 14 and Leviticus 11. Leviticus 11 is the more inclusive version. The Y'iddish word *kosher* is used to describe foods which are "clean" according to the Jewish ritual law. *Kashrut* refers to the total set of laws which, together, determine the foods that are "clean" or "unclean".

The Lord spoke again to Moses and Aaron, saying to them, "Speak to the sons of Israel, saying, 'These are the creatures which you may eat from all the animals that are on the earth. Whatever divides a hoof, thus making split hoofs, and chews the cud, among the animals, that you may eat. Nevertheless, you are not to eat of these, among those which chew the cud, or among those which divide the hoof: the camel, for though it chews the cud, it does not divide the hoof, it is unclean to you.

'Likewise, the rock badger, for though it chews the cud, it does not divide the hoof, it is unclean to you; *[It had to both chew the cud and divide the hoof]* the rabbit also, for though it chews cud, it does not divide the hoof, it is unclean to you; and the pig, for though it divides the hoof, it does not chew cud, it is unclean to you. You shall not eat of their flesh nor touch their carcasses; they are unclean to you.

'These you may eat, whatever is in the water: all that have fins and scales, those in the water, in the seas or in the rivers, you may eat.

'But whatever is in the seas and in the rivers, that do not have fins and scales *[in other words, shellfish]* among all the teeming life of the water, and among all the living creatures that are in the water, they are detestable to you, and they shall be abhorrent to you the *[notice the words 'detestable' and 'abhorrent'—they recur throughout this passage]*; you may not eat of their flesh, and their carcasses you shall detest.

'Whatever in the water does not have fins and scales is abhorrent to you. These, moreover, you shall detest among the birds; they are abhorrent, not to be eaten: the eagle and the vulture and the buzzard, and the kite and the falcon in its kind, every raven in its kind, and the ostrich and the owl and the seagull and the hawk in its kind, and the little owl and the cormorant and the great owl, and the white owl and the pelican and the carrion vulture, and the stork, the heron in its kinds, and the hoopoe, and the bat.

'All the winged insects that walk on all fours are detestable to you. Yet these you may eat among all the winged insects which walk on all fours: those which have above their feet jointed legs with which to jump on the earth.

'These of them you may eat: the locust in its kinds, and the devastating locust in its kinds, and the cricket in its kinds, and the grasshopper in its kinds. But all other winged insects which are four-footed are detestable to you.

'By these, moreover, you will be made unclean: whoever touches their carcasses becomes unclean until evening, and whoever picks up any of their carcasses shall wash his clothes and be unclean until evening.

'Concerning all the animals which divide the hoof, but do not make a split hoof, or which do not chew cud, they are unclean to you: whoever touches them becomes unclean.

'Also whatever walks on its paws, among all the creatures that walk on all fours, are unclean to you; whoever touches their carcasses becomes unclean until evening, and the one who picks up their carcasses shall wash his clothes and be unclean until evening; they are unclean to you.

'Now these are to you the unclean among the swarming things which swarm on the earth: the mole, and the mouse, and the great lizard in its kinds, and the gecko, and the crocodile, and the lizard, and the sand reptile, and the chameleon.

'These are to you the unclean among all the swarming things; whoever touches them when they are dead, becomes unclean until evening.

'Also anything on which one of them may fall when they are dead, becomes unclean, including any wooden article, or clothing, or skin, or a sack—any article of which use is made—it shall be put in the water and be unclean until evening, then it becomes clean.

'As for any earthenware vessel into which one of them may fall, whatever is in it becomes unclean and you shall break the vessel.

'Any of the food which may be eaten, on which water comes, shall become unclean; and any liquid which may be drunk in every vessel shall become unclean.

'Everything, moreover, on which any part of their carcass may fall becomes unclean; an oven or a stove shall be smashed; they are unclean and shall continue as unclean to you.

'Nevertheless, a spring or a cistern collecting water shall be clean, though the one who touches their carcass shall be unclean. And if a part of their carcass falls on any seed for sowing which is to be sown, it is clean. Though if water is put on the seed, and a part of their carcass falls on it, it is unclean to you.

'Also if one of the animals dies which you have for food, the one who touches its carcass become unclean until evening. He too, who eats some of its carcass shall wash his clothes and be unclean until evening; and the one who picks up its carcass shall wash his clothes and be unclean until evening.

'Now every swarming thing that swarms on the earth is detestable, not to be eaten. Whatever crawls on its belly, and whatever walks on all fours, whatever has many feet, in respect to every swarming thing that swarms on the earth, you shall not eat them, for they are detestable.

'Do not render yourselves detestable through any of the swarming things that swarm *[notice that if you eat it, you yourself become detestable]*; and you shall not make yourselves unclean with them so that you become unclean.

'For I am the Lord your God. Consecrate yourselves therefore, and be holy; for I am holy. And you shall not make yourselves unclean with any of the swarming things that swarm on the earth.

'For I am the Lord, who brought you up from the land of Egypt, to be your God; thus you shall be holy for I am holy.

'This is the law regarding the animal, and the bird, and every living thing that moves in the waters, and everything that swarms on the earth, to make a distinction between the edible creature and the creature which is not to be eaten'" *(Leviticus 11:1-47).*

A lack of food is famine. During the Inter-Testamental period the people had the Maccabees, but they had no prophets. There was no prophet from the time of Malachi to the time of John the Baptist. He came in the spirit of Elijah and fed God's people during a famine. So it will be before Jesus comes. There will be a famine for the hearing of the Word of God.

"Behold the days are coming," declares the Lord God, *"when I will send a famine on the land. Not a famine for bread or a thirst for water, but rather for hearing the words of the Lord."* (Amos 8:11) The way that Elijah fed the Gentile woman and her son is a type of the way the ministry of Elijah will operate in the last days.

Those dietary laws are interesting. *Jesus said, "What goes into a man's mouth does not make him 'unclean', but what comes out of his mouth, that is what makes him 'unclean'".* (Matthew 15:11).

In the ancient Near East, with its lack of refrigeration and a desert environment where animals scavenged to survive, there was a high risk of food poisoning. In particular, illnesses like trichinosis and botulism could be contracted from eating certain kinds of food. Pork or shellfish—not properly frozen, preserved or cooked, eaten in that kind of environment—was potentially deadly. So there was a legitimate medical reason not to eat these foods.

But in a famine, anthropologists tell us, even the most civilised of human beings will eat anything. There are case studies where survivors of a ship wreck, for example, have actually resorted to cannibalism, eating the flesh of their friends, even their own families.

Notice in verse 47, you are to "make a distinction" between that which is *kosher* and that which is not *kosher,* between the clean and the unclean, between the edible and that which is not to be eaten. The text continually reiterates that if something is not kosher, it is to be detestable, abhorrent, loathsome. The thought of eating them should make us feel sick. These things shall be abhorrent to you—rats, serpents, bats, roaches, they shall be abhorrent to you. Just think about eating something like that should make you feel sick. But in a famine people get hungry enough to eat anything. They will even devour each other.

In the beginning was the Word, and the word was with God, and he word was God... And the word (Logos) became flesh, and dwelt among us... (John 1:1,14).

The word for "dwelt" in Greek is *kataskenoo.* It is a Greek translation of the Hebrew verb "to tabernacle". The Hebrew is *mishkan* (from which comes *Shekinah*). *Mishkan* speaks of God's dwelling place. John is saying that the same God who was present with ancient Israel—the *Shekinah* who dwelt in the tabernacle, the *Mishkan*—had now become flesh. God had become a man.

The ancient Greeks were dualists. They understood about the 'Logos', the creative agent of God and even the salvific agent of God, but their concept of God was of a transcendent being. The Greeks could not handle the idea that "God became a man, the word became flesh". They believed that everything physical was bad; everything spiritual was good. Anything physical was regarded as the domain of a lesser god.

Notice how this perverts a biblical truth. The bible does not say everything physical is bad. It says everything physical is *fallen,* and has come under the domain of Satan, temporarily. Satan's lies always pervert a truth.

Amongst the Greeks there were two groups: the Stoics and the Epicureans. The Stoics would deny everything physical and live a monastic life, based on mortification of the flesh. The Epicureans lived a life of lasciviousness. They believed that only the spiritual realm mattered. Both groups taught that there was a split between the physical world and the spiritual world. John's teaching that God could become a man went directly against the dualistic Greek ideas.

Dualism has many forms. Christian Science is dualistic. What does Christian Science say? "My body is lying to me. This doesn't matter: it is only the physical, it is the spiritual that matters. Death is an illusion. Old age is an illusion." Mary Baker Eddy, the founder of Christian Science first fell victim to the illusion of old age, then she fell victim to the illusion of sickness, then—*voilà, la grande illusion*—she cashed in her chips! Men like E.W.Kenyon, Kenneth Hagin and Kenneth Copeland teach this same dualism, which they learned from Christian Science.

The bible says that we are called to be *in* the world, but *not of it* (John 15:18-19; 16:33; Romans 12:2; Galatians 6:14; James4:4, 1 John 2:15,27). We are not called to *be unnatural,* we are called to *be supernatural.*

The teaching that if God wants the spiritual man or the spiritual woman to suffer, they are happy to suffer, is not Christian. That is not natural, that is unnatural. That is *religious masochism.* Look at the example of Jesus. He said, "Father let this cup pass from me". He did not *want* to suffer but still said, "Thy will be done".

It is unnatural to say the spiritual believer *wants* to suffer, if that is the Lord's will. It is supernatural to say, "Lord, all things work together for good, and if You know this is the best thing, give me the grace to suffer". We are called to be natural. We are called to be supernatural. We are not called to be unnatural. The early church was up against this radical dualism, gnosticism, and all that went with it, and we have the same things today with the hyper-faith teachers.

The word became flesh (John 1:14). When Jerome translated the word "flesh" into Latin in the Vulgate, he did not use *corpus* (body), but *carnum,* meaning "meat". The Greek here is *sarx.* "*The word* (the logos) *became flesh* (sarx)", literally "became meat".

The Greek word for 'meat', *sarx,* is the same word for 'flesh'. The Hebrew word for 'meat', *basar,* is the same word for 'flesh'. The Latin word for 'meat', *carnum,* is the same word for 'flesh'.

Truly, truly I say to you, he who believes has eternal life. I am the bread of life. Your fathers ate the manna in the wilderness, and they died. This is the bread which comes down out of heaven, so that one may eat of it and not die. I am the living bread that came down out of heaven; if anyone eats of this bread, he shall live forever; and the bread also which I shall give for the life of the world is My sarx (John 6:47-51).

In the same way that "The Word became *sarx*", so now "The bread I give is my *sarx*—flesh".

The Jews therefore began to argue with one another, saying, "How can this man give us His flesh to eat?" (John 6:52). It is likely that those educated in midrash, the Sanhedrin, would have understood what he was on about.

Jesus therefore said to them "Truly I say to you, unless you eat the flesh of the Son of Man and drink His blood, you have no life in yourselves. He who eats My flesh and drinks My blood has eternal life, and I will raise him up on the last day. For My flesh is true food, and My blood is true drink. He who eat My flesh and drinks My blood abides in Me, and I in him. As the living Father sent Me, and I live because of the Father, so he who eats Me, he also shall live because of Me. This is the bread which came down out of heaven; not as the fathers ate, and died, he who eats this bread shall live forever" (John 6:53-58).

Jesus was talking about himself as *the bread that came down from heaven*. The manna in the wilderness was a type, Jesus is the anti-type.

We have to read the text in its context, but in turn we have to read that in the context of the whole bible. The rabbis tell us that the *matzoh*—the bread used as Passover—corresponds to the flesh of the lamb. The rabbis say it had to be striped and pierced because it corresponded to the flesh of the lamb. *But He was pierced through for our transgressions ... and with His stripes we are healed* (Isaiah 53:5). When Jesus stated that "the bread" was His flesh, He agreed with the rabbis. This relates to the Passover, in so far as passover also comes from the book of Exodus, where the manna began to fall.

The Roman Catholic church will try to tell you that the Lord's Supper is the key to eternal life, but that is absurd. In their catechism, the Roman Catholic church says that sins are forgiven by the sacraments of baptism and penance, not the eucharist, so they even contradict their own doctrine. (Roman Catholic doctrine always contradicts itself, as does Mormon doctrine).

For John 6:47-58 to be talking about the Lord's Supper, it would have had to be talking about the Last Supper, when the Lord's Supper was instituted. The Last Supper had to take place at Passover time in Jerusalem. The text tells us it was not yet passover, and this does not take place in Jerusalem. So it is not talking about the Last Supper, or the Lord's Supper in any primary sense.

What it is talking about is *the bread that fell in the wilderness*—a type of

Jesus—and He says this is His flesh. *Truly, truly, I say to you, he who believes has eternal life* (John 6:47). Believe equals "eat".

How do we get this? The word became flesh. The word, the *logos* became *sarx*. Eat the *sarx*, believe the word.

You must read the text in its context. It has nothing to do with the doctrine of transubstantiation, which is cannibalism, and it certainly has nothing to do with the Last Supper. Jesus said, *Do this in remembrance of me* (1 Corinthians 11:24-25). He used the language of the Hebrew memorial sacrifice.

The Roman Catholic mass is not the same sacrifice as Calvary. When you understand the Lord's Supper as a Jewish passover, it is a Jewish *zikharon* ("memorial"—see Exodus 12:14, 13:9, 17:14, 28:29; Leviticus 23:24; Numbers 5:15, 10:10; Joshua 4:7, etc)

Only when you divorce the Last Supper from its Jewish background can you begin to argue that it is the same sacrifice. But in the Jewish context that Jesus gave it, it cannot possibly be that. It is a memorial. *Do this in remembrance of Me*. It is a memorial of what Jesus did, in the same way that the passover meal is a memorial of that deliverance from Egypt.

The word becomes flesh. "Eat my flesh". What does that mean? It means "eat my word". You take it into yourself. This is not new, the prophets taught the same thing, and even afterwards it was the same with the apostles. *Thy words were found and I ate them* (Jeremiah 15:16).

You take it into yourself and you believe it. As Jesus said, He who believes eats my flesh.

"Now you, son of man, listen to what I am speaking to you; do not be rebellious like that rebellious house. Open your mouth and eat what I am giving you." Then I looked, behold, a hand was extended to me; and lo, a scroll was in it. When He spread it out before me, it was written on the front and on back; and written on it were lamentations, mourning and woe.

Then He said to me, "Son of man, eat what you find; eat this scroll, and go, speak to the house of Israel." So I opened my mouth, and He fed me the scroll. And He said to me, "Son of man, feed your stomach, and fill your body with this scroll which I am giving you." Then I ate it, and it was sweet as honey in my mouth (Ezekiel 2:8-3:3). Ezekiel ate the scroll. He ate the word of God.

And I went to the angel, telling him to give me the little book. And he said to me, "Take it, and eat it; and it will make your stomach bitter, but in your mouth it will be sweet as honey." And I took the little book out of the angel's hand and I ate it ... (Revelation 10:9-10).

Eat the word. That concept is in the Old Testament; it is in the New Testament. Jesus was teaching nothing new, only what the prophets said before Him, and what the apostles said after Him. *The word becomes flesh. Eat My word.* Belief equals "eat". The Word becomes flesh. His own substance, as God, becomes His Word.

Metabolically, what you eat you are. Jesus' essence - *His Word, His doctrine, His teaching*—is Himself. Whatever you eat becomes part of you. Thus, when you eat something spiritually, you become what you eat.

Terrestrial animals that the Jews were allowed to eat, that were *kosher* (clean), were types of Jesus Himself.

Lamb is *kosher. Behold the Lamb of God, who takes away the sins of the world* (John 1:29).

Goats are *kosher. But the goat on which the lot for the scapegoat fell, shall be presented alive before the Lord, to make atonement upon it, to send it into the wilderness as the scapegoat* (Leviticus 16:10).

Oxen are *kosher. And he sent the young men of the children of Israel, which offered burnt offerings, and sacrificed peace offerings of oxen...* (Exodus 24:4).

Every one of them, in some way or other, are types of Jesus. Eat what is kosher. Eat the word. If somebody is not kosher, keep away from them. Because if you begin eating *their* word, you are going to get sick. Eat what's healthy, eat what's clean. But if people become hungry enough—if there is a famine—people will eat *anything,* even each other.

We have to understand the Jewish idea of eating the flesh.

Concerning him (Melchizedek) *we have much to say, and it is hard to explain, since you have become dull of hearing* (Hebrews 5:11).

He is speaking here of *typology* and *midrash.* Melchizedek (Genesis 14:18-20; Psalm 110:4) is a christophany (a pre-incarnate manifestation of Christ), an Old Testament type of Jesus.

The writer is saying, "I am want to teach you typology and midrash, but you have lost the capacity to understand".

For though by this time you ought to be teachers, you have need again for someone to teach you the elementary principles of the oracles of God, and you have come to need milk and not solid food (meat). *For everyone who partakes only of milk is not accustomed to the word of righteousness, for he is a babe. But solid food is for the mature, who because of practice have their senses trained to discern good and evil* (Hebrews 5:12-14).

Again, he is saying, "I want to give you people meat. I want to teach you about the typology of Melchizedek, but I cannot. I have to teach you baby food. I cannot give you meat any more, I have to give you milk."

Therefore leaving the elementary teaching about the Christ, let us press on to maturity, not laying again a foundation of repentance from dead works and of faith towards God, of instructions about washings, and laying on of hands, and of the resurrection of the dead, and eternal judgement. And this we shall do if God permits (Hebrews 6:1-3).

We are in the same situation today. We need to go back and teach the basics. People have lost sight of the foundational doctrines like repentance, baptism, eternal judgement. People are saying that there is no hell. The church now needs milk, not meat, by and large.

And at this point, milk would be a big improvement. The Hindus actually drink cow urine because they think it is holy, and I know of Charismatics drinking the spiritual equivalent. Milk would be a big improvement.

Does that sound abhorrent? It is supposed to be abhorrent. *These shall be detestable to you.* The thought of it should make you feel sick.

But solid food is for the mature, who because of practice have their senses trained to discern good and evil (Hebrews 5:14).

They know how to put the word into effect; they have a discerning knowledge of the word and are able to put it into effect.

If people do not have an effectual knowledge of the word, they are not going to be discerning. When you are undiscerning, you will eat anything—kosher or not.

And I, brethren, could not speak to you as to spiritual men, but as to men of flesh, as to babes in Christ. I gave you milk to drink, not solid food; for you were not yet able to receive it. Indeed, even now you are not yet able, for you are still fleshly... (1 Corinthians 3:1-3).

Think of a baby when he learns to crawl, before he can walk. It does not matter what it is—a marble, a crayon, a tip of a pencil—as far as the child is concerned, it is a sweet, it is candy. The mother takes anything that could wind up in that kid's mouth, and puts it up where the kid cannot reach it. Because a baby is undiscerning, it will eat anything. So it is with

Christians who are not trained in right doctrine and the word of righteousness, they will eat anything (especially if they are hungry enough). Milk would be a big improvement. Paul is complaining, "I wish they would drink their milk, maybe then we could take them out for a steak."

Animals that do not chew the cud or split the hoof are not kosher. *Now these* [the Bereans] *were more noble-minded than those in Thessalonica, for they received the word with great eagerness, examining the Scriptures daily, to see whether these things were so* (Acts 17:11).

The Bereans chewed the cud.

Chewing the cud is not vomiting or regurgitating the food. It is bringing it up again, chewing over it, then swallowing it and taking it into your metabolism. Many Christians today have forgotten how to chew the cud. "Jacob Prasch or Derek Prince said it, so it must be true!" No, no, no. Paul said we should judge even what he taught (Galatians 1:8).

Jesus said, *But do not be called Rabbi; for One is your teacher and you are all brothers* (Matthew 23:8).

Chew the cud. Eat the food, bring it up again, pray about it, examine the scriptures and, then, if it is right, swallow it. Otherwise spit it out.

Beware of false prophets, who come to you in sheep's clothing, but inwardly are ravenous wolves (Matthew 7:15).

Wolves can imitate Christians. They can look like sheep, but they are false prophets. Their flesh (their teaching, their doctrine) is not kosher. Do not eat it. It should be abhorrent to you.

You serpents, you brood of vipers, how shall you escape the sentence of hell? (Matthew 23:33).

Satan is a deceiver; the serpent beguiled the woman, Eve—a type of Israel and the church. Religious leaders who teach false doctrines come in the character of serpents. Jesus says they will go to hell if they do not repent. (He uses the Greek subjunctive mood here. The subjunctive mood in Greek implies doubt. It's not important in English, but it's very important in Greek. What He is saying is, "It is possible for you not to go to hell, but it is very unlikely you're going to go anywhere but hell".)

Teachers of false doctrine crawl like snakes. They are deceptive, beguilers. They come in the character of serpents. Do not eat them. Keep away from people who teach spiritual seduction.

Can you picture yourself picking up a snake and eating it? Would you eat a viper? No! Well, keep away from those vipers and their teaching. Do not eat it. The word becomes flesh. Keep away.

Is eating a snake disgusting to you? The thought of eating a prosperity preacher's doctrine should be just as disgusting. When you see someone sitting down reading a book by a prosperity preacher, you should think of somebody munching on a rat! That is what they are doing. It shall be detestable to you, it shall be abhorrent. The thought of eating these vile, vermin-ridden animals is disgusting, and the thought of eating those false doctrines should be just as disgusting.

Wherever the corpse is, there the vultures will gather (Matthew 24:28). Vultures attack the Body. They prey on what is dead, on the persecuted church. Do not eat it! Vultures should be abhorrent to you. You will come across people who prey on dying bodies.

They find a church that is in trouble and come along claiming to be the miracle man who will turn the church around. But all they do is carry off a limb, or a foot, so they can begin their own thing somewhere. Vultures are not kosher. They should be abhorrent to you.

And they came to the other side of the sea, into the country of the Gerasenes. And when He had come out of the boat, immediately a man from the tombs with an unclean spirit met Him, and he had his dwelling among the tombs. And no one was able to bind him any more, even with a chain; because he had often been bound with shackles and chains, and the chains had been torn apart by him, and the shackles broken in pieces, and no one was strong enough to subdue him (Mark 5:14).

Super-human physical strength and super-human intellectual power are two characteristics that frequently accompanying demon possession. Adolph Hitler was a paper hanger, but look at the way he was able to incite a whole nation. Almost every recorded case of demon possession in the bible was accompanied by irrational behaviour - throwing themselves into fire, living in graves, etc.—Mary Magdalene and Judas being the notable exceptions. You can almost rule out demon possession in cases where there is no irrational behaviour.

And constantly night and day, among the tombs and in the mountains, he was crying out and gashing himself with stones. And seeing Jesus from a distance, he ran up and bowed down before Him; and crying with a loud voice, he said, "What do I have to do with You, Jesus, Son of the Most High God? I implore You by God, do not torment me!"

For He had been saying to him, "come out of the man, you unclean spirit?"
And He was asking him, "What is your name?"
And he said to Him, "My name is Legion; for we are many" (Mark 5:5-9).

Now, if you can believe it, there is a president of an Assemblies of God Bible College in Australia (Alun Davies) who wrote in an article in their magazine called *The Evangel* that the man's name, not the demon's, was "Legion."

This "president" is (supposedly) training others to be ministers. They will eat anything, won't they!

And he began to entreat Him earnestly not to send them out of the country. Now there was a big herd of swine feeding there on the mountain. And the demons entreated Him, saying, "Send us into the swine so that we may enter them." And He gave them permission. And coming out, the unclean spirits entered the swine; and the herd rushed down the steep bank into the sea, about two thousand of them; and they were drowned in the sea (Mark 5:10-11).

Pigs are not kosher. In Galilee, there were Gentiles and probably Jews who were not particularly observant, who would have kept pigs. To understand what is happening here, we have to understand the midrash.

Do not throw your pearls before swine, lest they trample them under their feet, and turn and tear you to pieces (Matthew 7).

Who are swine? People who mock and reject the gospel. What happens to them? *Then He will say to those on His left, "Depart from Me, accursed ones, into the eternal fire which has been prepared for the devil and his angels"* (Matthew 25:41).

And the devil who deceived them was thrown into the lake of fire... (Revelation 20:10).

In Mark chapter 5, the Sea of Galilee becomes a picture of the lake of fire. In Revelation, those who mock and reject the gospel go to the same place as the demons.

Look at fish. A marine biologist took me to a fantastic aquarium in Cape Town, South Africa. It is a tank constructed with actual chunks of the continental shelf, the under-water environment around South Africa. And they put the animals in there, like sharks, and you walk through glass tubes and can see the sharks swimming above you. It is really incredible. He was showing me around and I was looking at the shellfish. They are scavengers at the bottom of the sea and they eat garbage. They are not kosher. We are not to eat them.

They eat garbage, so – what you eat, you are—they become garbage.

And He said to them, "Follow Me, and I will make you fishers of men" (Matthew 4:19).

The apostles threw in the nets and pulled out fish when Jesus told them where to cast the nets. We can witness, witness, and witness, but until Jesus tells us where to cast our nets, you are not going to catch many fish. That is not to discourage personal witnessing or evangelism but, when we talk about mission programs or crusades, they have to be directed by the Holy Spirit, otherwise you are not going to catch many fish.

But what are shellfish like? The Book of Revelation speaks of *the earth* and *the sea* (Revelation 5:13; 7:1,2,3; 10:2,5,6,8; 12:12; 14:7).

There are two beasts, one from *the sea* (Revelation 13:1) and one from *the earth* (Revelation 13:11).

The earth speaks of Israel, *the sea* speaks of the nations. *Why are the nations in an uproar?* (Psalm 2:1).

Shellfish are closed and so far into the sea that they will not get caught in a net. Shellfish speak of people who are closed and who are filled with garbage. If you do not eat right food you are going to eat wrong food. They eat garbage and they become garbage. They are so far into the world system that they are not going to get saved. They are closed to the gospel. Do not eat them.

If one of these unclean animals fell on a seed before it was planted, the seed (and the fruit that came out of it) could be eaten.

And if a part of their carcass falls on any seed for sowing which is sown, it is clean (Leviticus 11:37).

Why?

Truly, truly, I say to you, unless a grain of wheat falls into the earth and dies, it remains by itself alone; but if it dies, it bears much fruit (John 12:24).

That which you sow does not come to life unless it dies... (1 Corinthians 15).

This is a catabolic process. When you plant the seed, it has the germ inside. The seed falls into the earth and dies. And a new creation comes out. So with us. The old creation is planted with Christ. We die with Him in baptism, we are buried with Him, and we are resurrected with Him. Our glorified bodies that are going to come out ultimately will be different to what went in. It does not matter what the seed does; it does not matter what the old creation did. You could have been a homosexual, a prostitute, a drug dealer, an alcoholic, a criminal—it does not matter what the old creation did, if it falls into the earth and dies, the food is clean.

The chameleon is not kosher.

What is a chameleon? The Hebrew word for "chameleon" is the same as the Hebrew word for "hypocrite". Do not eat it! Watch out for hypocrites.

For it is written in the Law of Moses, "You shall not muzzle the ox while he is threshing." God is not concerned about oxen, is He? Or is He speaking altogether for our sake? Yes, for our sake it was written, because the ploughman ought to plough in hope, and the thresher to thresh in hope of sharing the crops (1 Corinthians 9:9).

This is talking about those honest preachers who deserve to be paid for the ministry. Those who work hard at preaching and teaching the word of God, and teach it accurately and fairly, are the only ones who deserve the privilege of being paid for it. *Do not muzzle the ox when he is threshing.* The ox is clean; you can follow his teaching. You can eat the ox, but not the pig, not the serpent, not the wolf.

Doves are *kosher*—they are types of Jesus. They are one of the five creatures that God ordered Abraham to sacrifice (Genesis 15:9).

In the Law of Moses, they had to be sacrificed "over running water" (Leviticus 14:5), symbolising "the washing of water with the word" (Ephesians 5:26).

There were the clean and the unclean animals. Zoologically we do not know what all of the animals mentioned in Leviticus were.

Some may be extinct, some may no longer be indigenous to the Middle East, but those that we do know, or can find parallels of in the bible, all teach us something about our spiritual diet.

If people get hungry enough they will eat anything—mice, rats, bats, lizards, Kingdom-Now, Ecumenism, Name-it-and-Claim-it, Faith Prosperity. *It shall be abhorrent to you.* The bible keeps saying to you, over and over, *It shall be detestable to you.* These unclean spiritual foods should disgust you. The thought of them should be so disgusting to you that you have to put them out of your head, because it makes you sick. The idea of swallowing a Benny Hinn doctrine should be like the idea of eating a rat—it should make you feel sick.

It shall be abhorrent to you, it shall be detestable to you. The Book of Mormon—it shall be detestable to you. The Watchtower—it shall be detestable to you; it should make you feel sick. Keep away from them. If you eat their teaching you will become something disgusting and unholy in the sight of God.

When Elisha returned to Gilgal, there was a famine in the land. As the sons of the prophets were sitting before him, he said to his servant, "Put on the large pot and boil stew for the sons of the prophets" (2 Kings 4:38).

There is a famine in the land. There is nothing to eat, but the people have to eat something. *Then one went out into the field to gather herbs, and found a wild vine and gathered from it his lapful of wild vine gourds, and came and sliced them into the pot of stew, for they did not know what they were* (2 Kings 4:39).

When people are hungry enough, they will eat anything. *So they poured it out for the men to eat. And it came about as they were eating of the stew, that they cried out and said, "O man of God, there is death in the pot." And were unable to eat* (2 Kings 4:40).

There was death in the pot. You eat this stuff—this unkosher food, this pork or shellfish that has not been refrigerated – and you will die of botulism or trichinosis. There is death in it. So what did Elisha do?

But he said, "Now bring meal." [Bring the grain.] *And he threw it into the pot, and he said, "Pour it out for the people that they may eat." Then there was no harm in the pot* (2 Kings 4:41).

You put the grain in it. People who eat the grain are not going to get sick from eating this other stuff. They are not going to be affected by false doctrine and false teaching. They are not going to be sucked into ecumenism, Kingdom-Now theology, or Name-it-and-Claim-it.

The grain takes out the poison. The grain absorbs the toxins. The grain renders it harmless. True teaching renders false teaching harmless.

It shall be abhorrent to you. Rats, snakes, vermin—it should be abhorrent. False doctrine, and those who teach it, should be abhorrent. You should not even think of listening to those tapes, or going to those conferences, or reading those books, any more than you would munching on a rat. It should be abhorrent to you. But if people are hungry enough, they will eat anything!

This teaching is not some kind of poetic licence. Read what happened to the apostle Peter.

And on the next day, as they were on their way, and approaching the city, Peter went up to the house-top about the sixth hour to pray.

And he became hungry, and was desiring to eat; but while they were making preparations, he fell into a trance; and he beheld the sky opened up, and a certain object like a great sheet coming down, lowered by four corners to the ground, and there were in it all kinds of four-footed animals and crawling creatures of the earth and birds of the air (Acts 10:9-12).

The reference is to the foods mentioned in Leviticus 11 and Deuteronomy 14—foods that were not kosher and which should be abhorrent to him.

And a voice came to him, "Arise, Peter, kill, and eat!" But Peter said, "By no means, Lord, for I have never eaten anything unholy and unclean". (Acts 10:13-14)

In other words, Peter was saying, "I will not eat what is not kosher".

And again a voice came to him a second time, "What God has cleansed, no longer consider unholy." And this happened three times; and immediately the object was taken up into the sky (Acts 10:15-16).

And he [Peter] said to them, "You yourselves know how unlawful it is for a man who is a Jew to associate with a foreigner or to visit him; and yet God has shown me that I should not call any man unholy or unclean" (Acts 10:28).

The issue is the person and their beliefs, it is not race. The issue is what the person believes. The Romans of Peter's day worshipped other gods; they worshipped Jupiter and all the rest of the Roman pantheon.

Remember Jesus and the Syro-Phoenician woman who asked Jesus to heal her daughter. Jesus said, *"It is not good to take the children's bread and throw it to the dogs"* (Mark 7:27). What are "dogs"?

For dogs have surrounded me; a band of evildoers has encompassed me; they pierced my hands and feet (Psalm 22:16).

"Dogs" was a derogatory Jewish term for pagans. *"It is not good to take the children's bread and throw it to the dogs."*

He was not making a racist statement. Jesus loved that little Gentile girl as much as He would have loved a little Jewish girl. But what He was saying was, "Lady, your religion is not fit for human consumption. I am not going to give bread to 'dogs'. Become a human being."

In Peter's vision in Acts 10, what do the unkosher animals represent?

Pagans. Gentiles. Unbelievers. "Dogs". These were the unkosher animals of the vision.

"Peter, eat this, accept it, swallow it."

"Hey, wait a minute, there's a kosher 'deli' right down the street. I'm not touching this!" *"Peter, eat it!"*

God makes unclean people clean. He saved these Gentiles. He made them edible. He made their beliefs right. God can make anybody clean, even Christians who have gone into eating spiritual rats and cockroaches. God can make even them clean, if they repent.

When I was a little boy in New York, the monsoon rains failed to come to India in sufficient quantity one year and there was a famine in India. The second most populous country in the world was facing mass starvation. And there was a big campaign: "Must India Starve?" It was on billboards, in newspapers, on television. Magazines promoted the theme: "Must India starve?"

The wheat producing nations of the world - like Argentina, America, Canada, and Australia - donated large quantities of wheat. And people all over the world raised money. Christian farmers in the American Mid-west—a lot of them were believers—tithed their wheat to India, or to various Christian relief agencies.

Then a magazine in the United States came out with a full page spread. The heading at the top of the page said "Must India Starve?" And at the bottom of the page it said "Why Not?"

And there was a photograph of two Hindu boys - skinny little bags of bones, who were literally on the verge of dying of starvation, their bones popping out. The boys were holding a big sack of grain which had printed on the side, "United States Emergency Wheat—NOT FOR SALE—a gift from the people of America to the people of India." And while these two boys were holding the bag, a cow was eating the wheat!

False religion will always bring famine and death. Just look at the countries where these famines occur—it is concentrated in places like Latin America, Africa, and Asia where there is paganism, Catholicism and idolatry. I am not saying that Christians are immune from suffering, but one is a reflection of the other - they were hungry, they were starving to death, but there was food right in front of them.

The bible says *there will be a famine for the hearing of the word of God.*

There is already a famine, but it is going to get worse.

What would happen in a persecution if there were no bibles and no Christian meetings allowed, like in Saudi Arabia, or Iran? When that kind of persecution comes to countries like Britain or Australia or New Zealand, what are they going to do?

There is food all over the place now, but they are not eating it. What is going to happen when then is no food? Who is going to be the first to die? Those who refuse to eat the food that is in front of them will be the first to die.

It was a tragedy with those two Hindu boys starving in India. The tragedy was not simply that they were starving, but rather that they were starving with food right in front of them. The famine I see happening in the church today, where people are eating anything—literally anything, no matter how crazy, how sickening, how poisonous—is a tragedy. But the bigger tragedy is that there is still plenty of grain in the silo!

THE WOMAN OF SAMARIA

*W*HEN therefore the Lord knew that the Pharisees had heard that Jesus was making and baptizing more disciples than John (although Jesus was not baptizing, but his disciples were), He left Judea, and departed again into Galilee.

And He had to pass through Samaria. So he came to a city of Samaria, called Sychar, near the parcel of ground that Jacob gave to his son Joseph; and Jacob's well was there.

Jesus therefore, being wearied from His journey, was sitting thus by the well. It was about the sixth hour. There came a woman of Samaria to draw water. Jesus said to her, "Give me a drink." For His disciples had gone away into the city to buy food.

The Samaritan woman therefore said to Him, "How is it that You, being a Jew, ask me for a drink since I am a Samaritan woman?" (For Jews have no dealings with Samaritans.)

Jesus answered and said to her, "If you knew the gift of God and who it is that says to you, 'Give Me a drink,' you would have asked Him, and he would have given you living water." She said to Him, "Sir, you have nothing to draw with and the well is deep; where then do you get that living water? You are not greater than our father Jacob, are you, who gave us the well, and drank of it himself, and his sons and his cattle?"

Jesus answered and said to her, "Every one who drinks of this water shall thirst again; but whoever drinks of the water that I shall give him shall never thirst; but the water I shall give him shall become in him a well of water springing up to eternal life."

The woman said to him, "Sir, give me this water, so I will not be thirsty, nor come all the way here to draw."

He said to her, "Go, call your husband and come here." The woman answered and said, "I have no husband."

Jesus said to her, "You have well said, 'I have no husband'; for you have had five husbands, and the one whom you now have is not your husband; this you have said truly."

The woman said to Him, "Sir, I perceive that You are a prophet. Our fathers worshipped in this mountain, but you people say that in Jerusalem is the place where men ought to worship."

Jesus said to her, "Woman, believe me, an hour is coming when neither in this mountain, nor in Jerusalem, shall you worship the Father. You worship that which you do not know; we worship that which we know, for salvation is from the Jews.

"But an hour is coming and now is, when the true worshippers shall worship the Father in spirit and truth; for such people the Father seeks to be His worshippers. God is spirit, and those who worship Him must worship in spirit and truth."

The woman said to Him, "I know that Messiah is coming (He who is called Christ); when that One comes, he will declare all things to us." Jesus said to her, "I who speak to you am He."

And at this point His disciples came, and they marvelled that He had been speaking with a woman; yet no one said, "What do You seek?" or "Why do You speak with her?"

So the woman left her water pot, and went into the city, and said to the men, "Come, see a man who told me all the things I have done; this is not the Christ, is it?" They went out of the city and were coming to Him (John 4:1-30).

To understand the story of the woman at the well, we begin by looking at the well.

In biblical typology, different liquids typify the Holy Spirit in different aspects. New wine is a liquid which represents the Holy Spirit in the aspect of worship. Another liquid is oil, which speaks of the anointing of the Holy Spirit. But the living water, in scripture, is always the Holy Spirit *outpoured.*

Jesus explained it this way: *"He who believes in Me, as the scripture said, from his innermost being shall flow rivers of living water." But this He spoke of the Spirit whom those who believed in Him were to receive; for the Spirit was not yet given, because Jesus was not yet glorified* (John 7:38-39).

Jesus said directly that living water is the Holy Spirit outpoured.

The incident where Jesus taught about living water took place at Succoth—the Feast of Tabernacles or Booths (John 7:2,10). One of the regular events of that feast was the taking of water from the Pool of Siloam in a procession, lead by the Levites, to the Gabbatha where the water would be poured out on the stones. It was against this background that Jesus identified Himself as the One who would give living water to anyone who was thirsty and willing to come to Jesus to drink.

For I will pour out water on the thirsty land and streams on the dry ground; I will pour out My Spirit on your offspring and My blessing on your descendants (Isaiah 44:3).

The Holy Spirit is outpoured—the natural rain produces living water which goes into the water table.

Why is it that someone like Reinhard Bonnke has such tremendous success in Africa, but nothing much happens when he goes to Germany or England or Australia?

And furthermore, I withheld the rain from you while there were still three months until harvest. Then I would send rain on one city and on another city I would not send rain; one part would be rained on, while the part not rained on would dry up (Amos 4:7). There are many misguided evangelical church leaders in the world today who believe that, if they get the right program, they will get the right results.

Alpha courses, "purpose-driven church" models, the "Willow Creek" models of Bill Hybels and, most seriously, the ideas of C.Peter Wagner (ecumenist and Morris Cerullo advocate) of Fuller seminary effectively derive from this flawed and unbiblical notion.

This thinking comes from the church growth movement and is an example of people taking a high-tech world view and applying it the church. *Get the right software package for your hardware and your computer will do what you want.* They repackage their ecclesiology and missiology according to the pattern of our high-tech world, rather than according to scripture.

It is raining in Africa, it is raining in Brazil, it is raining in Indonesia; there is a drought in Britain and Australia. The bible says that, by God's direction, one place will be rained on, but another will not be rained on and dry up. The Holy Spirit must be outpoured. And it does not matter how many programs they have and how much money they spend, they are not going to make it rain. God is sovereign. He can be petitioned, but not manipulated.

Next we need to understand the Samaritans of Jesus' day. At that time, Jews had no dealings with Samaritans. In a similar fashion today, Protestants in Northern Ireland (for example) have no dealings with Catholics. The kinds of Jews who were around at the time of Jesus' first coming correspond convincingly to the kinds of Christians who are around today.

Sadducees: the Sadducees were anti-supernatural rationalists. They denied the resurrection, they denied the supernatural, denied angels, an afterlife and so on. Today we have Anglican bishops who deny the virgin birth and the resurrection. The Sadducees were very much akin to liberal Protestants.

Zealots/Herodians: then there were people who could not distinguish between their politics and their pulpit. The ones on the left were called Zealots. Josephus writes a lot about them. Some of Jesus' disciples were Zealots. Today it is called *liberation theology.* They say that the central event of the bible is not the resurrection of Jesus, but the exodus out of Egypt—because it was the political liberation of a nation and they combine that teaching with Marxist dialectics.

The left wing includes the Roman Catholic version in South America, or the liberal protestant version of Bishop Tutu and others in Africa. The ones on the right were called the *Herodians.* The equivalents today are the Dutch Reformed Church in South Africa, the fundamentalists in the American South, and the strict Presbyterians in Northern Ireland. They cannot distinguish between their political opinion and the bible.

Essenes: the third group were strange cults who knew something of Messianic significance was about to occur in Jewish history, but they cut themselves off from everyone else and developed strange beliefs concerning it. The foremost of these were the Essenes, who we know about from the Dead Sea Scrolls. Today there are all kinds of bizarre Adventist cults within Christianity.

Samaritans: when the ten northern tribes went into captivity, a small minority remained in Israel and intermarried with the Assyrians. These people mixed the bible with paganistic religion. They had a mountain other than Mount Zion, they had a kingship other than from the house of David, they had a priesthood other than the Levitical priesthood. They were descended from the people who opposed Ezra and Nehemiah in the rebuilding of the wall of Jerusalem and the temple. The Jews hated the Samaritans. They saw them as mongrelised Jews.

Today they are the Catholics, Anglo-Catholics and the Eastern Orthodox church; people who combine paganism with the bible. For example, the Roman Catholic church has a priesthood other than the Levitical priesthood, they have a separate holy city, and so on.

Most crucially, the Samaritans had a different doctrine of salvation. Under both the Old and New Covenant the key issue was: *How is sin atoned for?* In the Old Covenant, it was the temple, with the proper sacrifices conducted by the proper priests, at the proper time, and at the proper location. The Samaritans had a rival priesthood and a rival mountain. *How is sin atoned for?* They were not just arguing about real estate, they were arguing about soteriology, about salvation.

Pharisees: their doctrines were far better than everybody else, far closer to the truth. Jesus agreed with them on most issues. When He fought with the Sadducees, it was only because they gave Him a hard time. Normally he ignored the Sadducees. He dealt mainly with the Pharisees. There were two main groups of pharisees: the followers of the *School of Shammai* and the *School of Hillel*. St Paul came from the School of Hillel. The Pharisees were usually right on most things, but they had problems. One was the *oral law*—they took their tradition and gave it equal authority with scripture. Another problem was religious pride, which blinded them. And they were a materialistic aristocracy who, instead of feeding the sheep, used their position to aggrandise themselves. They understood midrash. They understood the *Seven Midroth* of Rabbi Hillel, who formulated them (though the contents had been around long before). They understood the deeper mysteries of the bible. Jesus said that the Pharisees had *"taken away* *the key to knowledge"* (Luke 11:52), the key to understanding these things.

The church over the centuries has lost this key to understanding. They are reading a Jewish book as if it were a Gentile one; they are reading a Hebraic book with a Hellenistic mind. The key is to go back to understanding the bible the way the apostles did, as a Jewish book.

You can see in the gospels that Jesus took the keys to understanding the scripture—which the Pharisees used to create a political, financial and social power base for themselves, to make themselves an elite, religious aristocracy—and gave them to the common people. That is why they hated Him. They should have been feeding the ordinary, common people, but they were not.

You can see this when Jesus, as a little boy, went to Jerusalem for his *bar mitzvah.* They were astounded. Where did he get this wisdom? How did this kid learn midrash? (Luke 2:47). Jesus gave the key to understanding the bible to the ordinary people.

For example, He reiterated the parable of the vineyard, from Isaiah 5:1-7, in Matthew 21:33-34. And it says, *When the chief priests and the Pharisees heard Jesus' parables, they knew he was talking about them*—because they knew the midrash. But he had to explain to His disciples privately what the parables meant. That is why the Pharisees hated Him: Jesus was showing all their cards.

In the same way, today, that you will not find a strict Presbyterian minister—in his orange sash and bowler hat—walking down the road in catholic West Belfast, you normally would not find a Jewish rabbi walking through Samaria. A Jewish rabbi returning from Jerusalem at Passover time, on his way back to Galilee, passing through Samaria, would have been doing the same thing. It went against everything they believed. To this day, Orthodox Jews pray, *Thank God I was not born a dog, a Gentile or a woman.*

(If you think Christianity and Judaism is sexist, you should see what it replaced in the pagan world—women were property, or less.) Jesus went against every social convention to make Himself known to this woman. He was more open, more loving, more caring, and more direct with her, and revealed more about Himself to her, than He did to His own Jewish disciples, at this point. He told her directly that He was the Messiah.

And He wanted to give her 'living water.' The idea here is midrash. What Jesus was doing was drawing on Jeremiah 2:13. *For My people* [the

Jews] *have committed two evils: they have forsaken Me, the fountain of living waters, to hew for themselves cisterns, broken cisterns, that hold no water.*

Jeremiah predicted that the Jews would commit two evils. The first evil is that they would reject the Messiah, the fountain of living water, the One who would give the Holy Spirit. The second evil is that they would create another religion, one that could hold no water, a broken cistern. The Jewish religion of today, Rabbinic Judaism, is not the Judaism of Moses and the Torah.

There is no temple, there is no priesthood; it is a religion invented by man, which has developed over a period of centuries. Much the same as Roman Catholicism is not the Christianity of the New Testament, Rabbinic Judaism is not the Judaism of the *Tenach*. On the roof of every Orthodox synagogue is the term *ichabod*—'the glory has departed'. They know the temple has been destroyed. Jewish Christians eat the Passover with lamb. They can do that because they still have a High Priest. His name is *Yeshua*. Orthodox Jews and other Jews will eat it with poultry, as a testimony to the fact that they cannot keep the Passover properly.

It says in Daniel 9:26 that the Messiah would come and die before the second temple would be destroyed. That is where Old Testament Judaism ended. We read in the *mishnah* that a scarlet cord hung before the Holy of Holies on Yom Kippur. If the scarlet cord turned white, the people's sins had been forgiven. We are told that for forty years before the temple was destroyed, the cord did not turn white. In other words, after the time of Jesus, the sins of the Jewish people were not forgiven. (That is in the *mishnah;* the rabbis admit that.) They are under the curse of the law.

Another religion was begun in Yavneh (a town in Israel) by Rabbi Yohanan ben Zaccai, a classmate of Rabbi Sha'ul of Tarsus (St Paul) in the School of Hillel, which was taught by Rabbi Gamaliel (the grandson of Rabbi Hillel). There were a number of famous rabbis in that school at that time. Another one was Rabbi Onkelos, who did some Targumim translations of the bible. But, undoubtedly, the two most famous of these rabbis were Rabbi Yohanan ben Zaccai and Rabbi Sha'ul of Tarsus. Every Jew would follow one of these two rabbis after the temple was destroyed.

At that time, Rabbi Yohanan ben Zaccai began the germ of what evolved into Rabbinic Judaism, where the rabbi would replace the Levitical priesthood, the synagogue would replace the temple, and where tradition and extra-biblical writings would begin taking the place of much of the Torah.

Rabbi Yohanan ben Zaccai was known as the "Mighty Hammer". At the end of his life, when he was on his deathbed, his disciples came and found him weeping. They asked him why he was weeping and he replied, "I am about to meet *Ha Shem,* blessed be His name, and there are two roads before me - one to paradise and one to gehenna. And I do not know to which of these two roads he will sentence me. That's why I'm weeping." The founder of Rabbinic Judaism said he had no assurance of salvation when he died. But his classmate, Rabbi Sha'ul of Tarsus said, *"The time of my departure has come ... in the future there is laid up for me a crown of righteousness, which the Lord, the righteous Judge, will award me on that day..."* (2 Timothy 6-8).

In the Jewish way of looking at the bible, when two things happen at the same geographical location, there is usually a theological and spiritual connection between them. For instance, King David was born at Bethlehem; Jesus, the 'Son of David' was born at Bethlehem. Elijah, Elisha and John the Baptist all had the same spirit. Elijah ended his ministry on the plain of Jericho, Elisha began his ministry on the plain of Jericho and the ministry of John the baptist took place on the plain of Jericho.

A first century Christian would have sought to understand John chapter four by considering the stories of a woman at the well in the Old Testament. Midrash asks, *Where has this happened before? How is it fulfilled in Jesus?* We never base doctrine on type or allegory. We use type and allegory to demonstrate doctrine that is elsewhere plainly stated in scripture. We are not gnostics, thank God. We are people who respect the Word of God. Whenever you see something happening in midrash, you need to go back and see where it happened before. When Abraham was old, he sent a servant to get a bride for his son (Genesis 24). He placed gifts of jewellery on a train of camels to be given to his kinsmen, to prove that he was sent by Abraham. The father sent a servant to prepare a bride for his son. God sent the Holy Spirit to prepare a bride for Jesus. This is a picture of the tri-unity of the godhead.

The servant prayed that he would be guided in finding God's appointed bride for Isaac.

And it came about before he had finished speaking, that behold, Rebekah who was born to Bethuel the son of Milcah, the wife of Abraham's brother Nahor, came out with her jar on her shoulder And the girl was very beautiful, a virgin, and no man had laid with her; and she went down to the spring [a well] and filled her jar, and came up. Then the servant ran to meet her, and said, "Please let me drink a little water from your jar."

At first Laban, Rebekah's brother, was suspicious of the servant but, when he saw the presents, he was convinced.

Then the girl ran and told her mother's household about these things. Now Rebekah had a brother whose name was Laban; and Laban ran outside to the man at the spring. And it came about that when he saw the ring, and the bracelets on his sister's wrists, and when he heard the words of Rebekah his sister, saying, "This is what the man told me," he went to the man; and behold, he was standing by the camels at the spring. And he said, "Come in, blessed of the Lord! Why do you stand outside since I have prepared the house, and a place for the camels?" (Genesis 24:28-31).

The gifts were given to prove that the servant was sent to get a bride for the son.

This story of a woman at a well resurfaces in John, with another woman who says, *"Jacob... gave us this well and drank of it himself..."* (John 4:12).

And he [Jacob] looked, and saw a well in the field, and behold, three flocks of sheep were lying there beside it, for from that well they watered the flocks.

Now the stone on the well was large. When all the flocks were gathered there, they would then roll the stone from the mouth of the well, and water the sheep, and put the stone back in its place on the mouth of the well. And Jacob said to them, "My brothers, where are you from?" And they said, "We are from Haran." And he said to them, "Do you know Laban the son of Nahor?" "We know him." And he said to them, "Is it well with him?" And they said, "It is well, and behold, Rachel his daughter is coming with the sheep. And he said, "Behold, it is still high day; it is not time for the livestock to be gathered. Water the sheep, and go, pasture them." But they said, "We cannot, until all the flocks are gathered, and they roll the stone from the mouth of the well; then we water the sheep" (Genesis 29:2-8).

Not until the resurrection, and the stone is rolled away, is the Spirit given. Jacob was involved with two women. He desired Rachel, but he did not get Rachel at first; he got Leah—the one he did not come for. It was only after he learned to love Leah as much as he loved Rachel, that he got

Rachel. In the beginning, Leah had all the babies; in the end, Rachel's womb became fruitful.

Jesus came for the Jews (John 1:11), but He would not get the Jews until He took the Gentile church and loved them as much as He loves Israel and the Jews. Then, as it says in Romans 11, the Jews will turn back to Him and He will get Israel. In the beginning, the Gentile church had all the babies. In the end, Israel will become a fruitful vine (Romans 11:25-26).

The Book of Ruth is read in the synagogue at *Shavuot* (the Feast of Weeks—Pentecost). Ruth tells the story of a rich man who takes a Gentile bride, and a child called Redeemer is born in Bethlehem. *And the people said to Boaz, "May the Lord make the woman who is coming into your house like Rachel and Leah, both of whom built the house of Israel"* (Ruth 4:11). This is because the church is to be made up of both Jew and Gentile.

There is a phenomenon in John's gospel which begins with Nathaniel, then Nicodemus, and which recurs throughout John. Jesus spoke on a spiritual plane—*You must be born again*—but the people listened to Him on a natural plane—*How can a man enter again into his mother's womb?* There are examples of this throughout John's gospel. It occurs in the other gospels as well and throughout scripture generally, but John's gospel is the place among the New Testament books where it is most conspicuous.

Jesus healed the paralytic by the Pool of Bethseda and told him, *"Pick up your pallet and go your way"* (John 5:8). If the guy had been healed and no longer needed the pallet, why did Jesus say "Pick up the pallet?" Because the pallet is a type of the cross—the thing to which he was to keep his flesh confined. In other words, Jesus was saying midrashically, in figure, *"Take up your cross and follow Me. Go the way of the cross"*.

Jesus frequently spoke on a spiritual level to people who were thinking on a physical level. So it was with the woman at the well. When Jesus met her, he broke every social convention in showing her recognition at all. And he began revealing things about Himself to her that He had not revealed to His disciples yet. Jesus showed great love and acceptance to a woman who Jews would have considered immoral, and a Samaritan on top of it!

They began to talk. She seemed to believe most of the things that Jews believed. She believed in the patriarchs—*"Our father Jacob"*. She believed in the Torah. (The Samaritans didn't hold the entire bible to be canonical, but they held to the Torah.) She believed the Messiah was coming, the same as the Jews. Ultimately she even believed that Jesus was the Messiah, apparently.

Some people would say, *"That is good enough. They've got the bible, they believe in the patriarchs, they believe in Jesus. That is good enough!"* But as soon as she began, *"Our fathers have this mountain, you have that mountain,"* what did Jesus do? The issue is not real estate, or some peripheral issue, the issue is central: Where is sin atoned for? How is sin atoned for?

The Roman Catholic church teaches that salvation comes primarily from the sacraments of *baptism* and *penance*. This is called sacramentalism and baptismal regeneration.

Salvation does not come by the sacraments. It comes by being born again. *But even though we, or an angel from heaven, should preach to you a gospel contrary to that which we have preached to you, let him be accursed* (Galatians 1:8).

Paul is saying, get away from such people. Have nothing to do with them. Even if they are an angel of God, reject them.

When Moses struck the rock (Exodus 17:6), and the living water flowed, it was like Jesus being crucified and the Holy Spirit being given. When Moses struck the rock more than once (Numbers 20:11), he was not able to enter the Promised land. It was counted a great sin. It was like crucifying Jesus again. The Roman Catholic church beats the gehenna out of the thing every time they have a mass. They say that, in the mass, Jesus dies again and again and again.

We have a High Priest who does not need daily, like those high priests [under the Old Covenant] *to offer up sacrifices, first for his own sins, and then for the sins of the people, because this He did once for all when He offered up Himself* (Hebrews 7:27).

Jesus died once. Not daily, like the Roman Catholic church teaches in the doctrine of the mass—they say it is the same sacrifice, that Christ dies sacramentally.

Not through the blood of goats and calves, but through His own blood, He entered the holy place once for all, having obtained eternal redemption (Hebrews 9:12)

For by one offering He has perfected for all time those who are sanctified (Hebrews 10:14).

Satan will always try to get Christians to deny the sufficiency of the cross in some way. Every perversion of Christianity will deny the cross in some way. Every deception will try to get you, the believer, away from the cross in its totality and sufficiency.

The *prosperity preachers* (Hagin, Copeland, etc.) teach that Jesus descended into hell became one nature with Satan and was born again in hell. That is where He won the victory. And because the cross is not central to their view of salvation, the cross is not central to their view of the Christian life, as in picking it up and following Jesus and living a crucified life.

The *Jehovah Witnesses* call it a "torture stake." They do not even want to call it a cross. They believe salvation comes through their organisation. Much of what is taught in the areas of "Inner Healing" and "Deliverance" is a subtle form of spiritual seduction, designed to deny the sufficiency of the cross. These people find someone and claim their great grandmother was a witch, or something, and tell them that they have to be delivered and set free from that thing.

All inner healing in the bible is predicated on two things: the first is forgiveness and the second is the cross. No matter what anybody did to me, I did worse things to God. No matter how I was hurt or rejected, I did worse to God. He is willing to forgive me, and I want Him to forgive me, but His condition is that I ask Him for the grace and strength to forgive others. That is the first basis of Christian inner healing.

The second is, *Consider yourselves to be dead to sin, but alive to God in Christ Jesus* (Romans 6:11). You have been crucified with Christ; you are a new creation. That abused child, that rejected wife, that whatever, is dead. You are a new creation. *Therefore if any man is in Christ, he is a new creature; the old things passed away; behold, new things have come* (2 Corinthians 5:17).

The devil will always try to get you to deny the sufficiency of the cross; to dig up the old man or the old woman and live with it in some way. I am not suggesting that people who come from these backgrounds do not need counselling and restoration and help in various ways. They do. But what they need must always be based on those two principles: forgiveness and the cross.

Jesus and the woman at the well were not simply arguing about *we had this mountain and you had that mountain.* The questions are: where is sin atoned for? and, how (on what basis) are we forgiven? Before He went any further in the conversation, He told her: *Lady, I like you. I am going against every social convention in speaking to you—because you are a Samaritan, you are a woman, you are supposedly a prostitute. I am breaking all the rules in talking to you, but I have to tell you something. Salvation comes from the Jews.*

Spirit AND truth. She had the right spirit, but she did not have the truth. Perhaps the Pharisees had the truth, but they did not have the right spirit. It is relatively easy for God to take someone who has the right spirit and give them the truth; it is usually more difficult to take someone who has the truth and give them a right spirit.

You can see this with very Calvinistic people and the attitudes they have. The predestination thing, and their elitist mentality often translates into racism. Practically everywhere there has ever been a hyper-Calvinistic church, there has been a history of injustice. The American South, with the segregation and the slavery—hyper-Calvinism; the Dutch Reformed Church and *apartheid* in South Africa—hyper-Calvinism; the strict Presbyterians in Northern Ireland—hyper-Calvinism. It goes all the way back to Calvin's police state in Geneva.

Jesus took the same attitude toward the woman at the well as he did to the Syrophoenician woman with the demon-possessed daughter. *"It is not good to take the children's bread and throw it to the dogs"* (Mark 7:27).

On the surface, that sounds like a very racist statement, but I assure you that Jesus loved that little Syrophoenician girl just as much as He loved any little Jewish girl. But what He was saying to that woman was, "Your religion is not fit for human consumption. I cannot give you what I have as long as you believe that stuff." Before He went any further in the conversation, He corrected her wrong religion. "Your religion is for dogs, not for humans". The Greek text is diminutive, actually means "little dogs".

Roman Catholicism is for dogs; it is not for human beings. It is idolatry. Praying to the dead is an abomination. Salvation does not come by the sacraments, it comes by the blood of Jesus being shed on the cross on our behalf. Spirit AND truth. It is not good enough to have the truth, if you do not have the right spirit. Neither is it good enough to have the right spirit, if you do not have the truth.

What did Jesus say? *Lady, salvation comes from the Jews. You do not know what you are talking about. They have the truth.* Salvation comes from evangelicals; not from Rome. There are many Roman Catholics like this woman at the well. They have the right spirit. When the Jews began rejecting the apostles in the book of Acts, many Samaritans began opening to the gospel. And many Roman Catholics are open today.

It is in Roman Catholic countries that God is working. While pentecostals are declining in Great Britain, Catholics are coming to Christ in the millions in Italy, Haiti, Philippines, and Brazil. In Europe, it is the Eastern Orthodox countries and Roman Catholic countries that never had the Reformation, where the church is beginning to grow. In Ireland today, more Catholics are coming to Christ than Protestants. The same is occurring in Italy, Spain, Portugal, Romania, Albania, Russia—countries that never had the Reformation, that is where the gospel is going.

Where is the church declining? England, Wales, Scotland, Holland, Germany, Switzerland, Scandinavia—places that have had the truth for centuries.

The Catholics have a right spirit and they want the truth. They are hungry. God loves the catholic people. They represent the future. Protestantism is the past. In Santiago, Chile, twenty thousand people get saved every week and leave the Roman Catholic church. In the Philippines it is the same. In Guatemala, ten per cent of the population left the Roman church over a period of ten years. That is why the Pope keeps going back there with his little tap dance: *Ave Maria, Gee its good to see ya, Please don't leave.*

What did Jesus say? Did He speak about Catholics the same way as Michael Harper or George Carey or the late John Wimber? *"It is okay if you pray to the dead. It is okay if you have another doctrine of salvation. As long as you believe in the bible and you believe in Jesus, that is good enough."*

No, it was not good enough. Salvation comes from the Jews. It is not that mountain, that is not the way your sins are going to be forgiven. It is not the sacraments. That is what Jesus said. And if we love catholic people, that is what we should say.

Now when the enemies of Judah and Benjamin heard that the people of the exile were building a temple to the Lord God of Israel they approached Zerubbabel and the heads of the fathers households, and said to them, "Let us build with you, for we, like you, seek your God, and we have been sacrificing to Him since the days of Esarhaddon king of Assyria, who brought us up here." But Zerubbabel and Jeshua and the rest of the heads of the fathers households of Israel said to them, "You have nothing in common with us in building a house to our God..." (Ezra 4:1-3).

What does the ecumenical movement say?

"Come, let us build with you. We are all one. We believe in Jesus. We have one bible. We believe what you believe. We are against abortion, too. We are against homosexuality, too [even though many of our priests are homosexuals].*"*

Hezekiah was a good king, but he made a terrible mistake—he showed his treasures to the king of Babylon. And the king of Babylon, as Jeremiah predicted, came and took them. When you see evangelicals showing their treasures to Rome, you can be sure that those treasures are going to be carried away one day. All the Roman Catholic literature on ecumenism says the same thing, that it is the road back to Rome. They openly admit it. It is only the silly Protestants who do not know any better. The present Pope says he wants to see one Europe with one church—the Roman Catholic church. We are told by people who promote ecumenism that this is the way to bring revival, or it is the way to see Roman Catholics saved. But if you look at the places where Roman Catholics are being saved (like Brazil, or Mexico, or the Philippines), they are all coming out of Rome. Those people will tell you, "We have left Babylon. Now we are Christians."

In February of 1999 speaking in Mexico, Pope John Paul II instructed Catholics to rise up against [evangelical] Protestants. In rural Mexico, churches are burned and Christians persecuted, yet ecumenical evangelical leaders like Chuck Colson did not complain.

It is only in post-Christian societies, with a charismatic movement which is no longer based on scriptural truth (if it ever was), and with leaders who either do not know the Word of God or who do not care about it; that you find the heresy of ecumenism being embraced.

"Let us build with you," they say. But Zerubbabel and Jeshua said, *"You have no part in building the city of our God."*

Remember that Roman Catholicism is based on gnosticism. Whenever you deal with a gnostic, you will find they use the same terms you do, but mean something different by them. For instance, when you talk to someone in the New Age (which is essentially gnostic), you might say, *"I saw the light"*. And they will tell you, *"I saw the light, too."* Only, you have one definition of the light, which is Jesus (John 1:9), and they have a different definition, which is the cosmic illumination of the inner self, but you both "saw the light."

When the Restoration people use words like "kingdom" and "victory," they mean different things by those terms than the bible does.

At an ecumenical forum with Roman Catholic and protestant theologians, the protestant theologian will say, "We are saved by grace". And the catholic theologian will agree, "Yes, we are saved by grace." Now the English word "grace" means "undeserved favour". The Hebrew word for grace is *chesed,* it means God's mercy in the covenant. The Greek word for "grace" is *charis,* meaning "gift." So, when the evangelical is thinking about, "We're saved by grace", they are thinking of God's gift, God's mercy in the covenant, or God's undeserved favour. To Roman Catholicism, "grace" is an ethereal substance earned by the sacraments. So they can both agree, "We are saved by grace," but they have two very different definitions of what that term actually means.

Spirit AND truth. The woman took Jesus' words about the living water on board. *So the woman left her water pot, and went into the city, and said to the men, "Come, see a man who told me all the things that I have done; this is not the Christ, is it?"* (John 4:28).

She left her water pot after she met Jesus and went to the people in the city. She left her religion, but not the people in it. Converted Roman Catholics should leave the Roman Catholic church, but not the people in it.

Salvation does not come by the sacraments. You must be born again. The Roman Catholic church is leading millions of people into hell by teaching that salvation comes through the sacraments. Praying to Mary is praying to the dead—it is an abomination to God. In the rosary, for every prayer said to God, a person says ten prayers to Mary—*blessed art thou among women...* Yes she was. *But Holy Mary mother of God?* That is not in the bible. It is blasphemy.

Pray for us sinners now, and at the hour of our death? That is putting Mary in the place of Jesus. The bible says that there is *ONE mediator between God and men, the man Christ Jesus* (1 Timothy 2:5). The bible says that Jesus alone is the Redeemer. Rome teaches that Mary is the co-redeemer. This all comes from the Babylonian cult religions, it is not from the bible.

There are Roman Catholic people who love Jesus and who are really seeking God. If somebody has the right spirit, they will take the truth. If they have the wrong spirit, they will not accept it.

The Roman Catholic Cardinal, *Edward Manning (1808-92)*, said in his autobiography that, as a priest, he knew of thousands of reasons why people became Roman Catholics. But he only knew of one reason why someone would leave the Roman Catholic church—that was because they had read the Word of God and ended up with more questions than any priest could ever possibly hope to answer.

Scholars say that at least seventy per cent of the Roman ritual is of pagan origin. *Cardinal John Henry Newman (1801-1900)*, in his treatise *The Development of the Christian Religion,* stated that "Temples, incense, oil lamps, votive offerings, holy water, holy days and seasons of devotion, processions, blessing of fields, sacerdotal vestments, the tonsure (of priests, monks and nuns), images, etc., are all of pagan origin" (p.359).

Two of their greatest, theologians, *Thomas Aquinas* and *Augustine of Hippo* denied the immaculate conception of Mary.

When you see people in the Roman church who claim to be born again, who will not leave when they are shown the truth, they were either not saved to begin with or they are backslidden into rebellion.

All over the world there are Roman Catholic men and women at the well. They are waiting for Jesus. They are waiting for us.

BINDING AND LOOSING

Y OU cannot eat soup with a fork! If you picked up a fork, how much soup do you think you would be able to eat with it? Not too much. You could try, but it would not work. Put down the fork, and pick up a spoon. Use the right utensil—and you will be able to eat the soup.

Today, we have an emphasis on *Spiritual Warfare.* The Lord has given us a lot of weapons and strategies, a lot of battle tactics and utensils to achieve the things we are called to do. But people are using the wrong weapons to deal with the subjects of the flesh, the devil and the world. You would think after a few minutes of eating the soup with a fork, people would have the sense to realize that something is wrong - this is not working, I must have something wrong.

In many areas the church is trying to use biblical teaching about *binding and loosing* as an instrument to deal with something it was not designed to deal with. They are using the wrong instrument, something that could never possibly achieve what they are thinking or hoping it can. There is a biblical teaching about binding and loosing, and it is the appropriate teaching, weapon and strategy for what it was designed to deal with. But principalities? Powers in the heavenlies? Sin? Wickedness in high places and in the world? It was not designed to deal with those things! We have been trying to eat soup with a fork!

After thirty years the charismatic renewal has failed to deal with the moral landslide of our society. Instead, the new age movement has now replaced Christianity as the spiritual consciousness of western society. The charismatic movement has failed to bring about revival. We have more crime, divorce, homosexuality, abused children, more substance abuse, and we have more of everything bad or evil now than we did thirty years ago, before the (so-called) charismatic renewal.

The church itself is far weaker and is in far worse shape spiritually and doctrinally now than it was thirty years ago. And still there you see us, with the fork, trying to eat the soup. We are still using the same silly instruments wrongly. A person with reasonable intelligence would know there is something wrong. There is nothing wrong with binding and loosing. It is not the instruments and utensils that are at fault.

In those days, I Daniel, had been mourning for three entire weeks. I did not eat any tasty food, nor did meat or wine enter my mouth, nor did I use any ointment at all, until the entire three weeks were *completed* (Daniel 10:2-3). Daniel fasted for three weeks. An angel came, and Daniel fell down terrified. *But I heard the sound of his words; and as soon as I heard the sounds of his words, I feel into a deep sleep on my face, with my face to the ground* (Daniel 10:9).

He was not rolling on the floor in hysterics, like you see with Toronto. He had nothing at all to do with what they call "slain in the spirit". Both Daniel and John were terrified. The people fell backwards when they came to arrest Jesus, all the other times, they went forwards.

The angel said, "O *Daniel, man of high esteem, understand the words that I am about to tell you and stand upright, for I have now been sent to you." And when he had spoken this word to me, I stood up trembling. Then he said to me, "Do not be afraid, Daniel, for from the first day that you set your heart on understanding this and on humbling yourself before your God, your words were heard, and I have come in response to your words. But the prince of the kingdom of Persia was withstanding me for twenty-one days; then, behold, Michael one of the chief princes, came to help me, for I had been left there with the kings of Persia"* (Daniel 10:11-12).

The bible always connects the spiritual battles in heaven with what you see on earth. In the vision of Zechariah, the high priest was standing before the angel of the Lord and Satan was standing before the throne making accusations (Zechariah 3:1). Same with Job (Job 1:9-11). Whatever was occurring in the heavens was reflected in what was happening on the earth.

Now Satan was cast down on the earth. Revelation records a battle happening in the heavens and the same going on in the earth. This always happens in spiritual warfare. The bible uses the term "principalities"; it does not say *territorial spirits,* although you could use that term. Daniel saw a demonic force over modern day Iran—the "prince of Persia." In the district of Gerasenes, when Jesus cast the demons out of the demoniac, the demons said, "don't send us out of the region" (Mark 5:1, Luke 8:26). These spirits are territorial, they have specific areas as their principality.

There is a biblical basis for this, but how do we deal with it? First, let us understand how we do not deal with it. I have no doubt that the same spiritual force is at work behind Iran today as that which Daniel saw. But Christians read a book by C.Peter Wagner and decide to take authority over that same spirit. And they believe that the problem will go away in three seconds. They think it is that easy. No, it is not that easy. Demons are powerful. Some are more powerful than others, Jesus said, *"This kind only goes by prayer and fasting"* (Matthew 17:21).

The church today labours under the burden of unbiblical ideas. Before we find out what is biblical, let us find out what is not biblical. Let us find out what the bible says about binding and loosing.

Acts chapter 17 tells the story of Paul in Athens. Athens was the European centre of pagan religion. Rome looked to Athens for its culture, for its religious ideas and for its philosophy. Pagan religion started with Nimrod in Babylon, made its way through Pergamum into Greco-Roman cultures, and from there into western culture.

Now while Paul was waiting for them at Athens, his spirit was being provoked within him as he was beholding the city full of idols (Acts 17:16). He was seeing the temples of the demons, and their places of worship.

So he was reasoning in the synagogue with the Jews and the God-fearing Gentiles, and in the marketplace every day with those who happened to be present

(Acts 17:17). "Those who happened to be present" included followers of Zeus, Apollo, Artemis, Astarte, Hermes, and so on. These people were all under the influence of demons.

What did Paul do? Did he recite the formulas taught by John Dawson and C.Peter Wagner: "I bind you, I loose you, I take authority over you in the name of Jesus"?

There are people in "deliverance ministry" who use this formula to save face and fortune. Their 'ministry' and income depends on forgetting the fact that it does not work. This is a deception which is known as *Dominionism,* or *Triumphalism,* or *Kingdom-Now* theology. The idea that we are going to conquer the world for Jesus Christ before He comes back and set up His kingdom is bogus. The idea that we can use the principles of the scriptures and the prayers of the saints to bring a moral influence into our fallen world and set up the kingdom of Jesus is absurd. Any time God's law has been used to reconstruct society, it has brought spiritual and theological death to the church, and general decline to society, government and culture.

Jesus' kingdom is not of this world (John 18:36). The two hyper-charismatic extremes—taking control of the planet, on one side, and withdrawing into a bunker out of fear, on the other—are the central pillars on which most of this error was built. There are times when the door of the ark is closed (Genesis 7:16), and there are times when we can only strengthen the things that remain (Revelation 3:2). But we are not supposed to go on the defensive in these last days. On the contrary, we are supposed to be happy, looking up, for our redemption draweth nigh (Luke 21:28). Before the end, the gospel of the kingdom must first be preached to every nation (Matthew 24:14).

Paul preached the gospel in the shadows of the demons at Athens. The first weapon to overrule the powers of darkness in our society is evangelism: we are to reason the gospel and to witness of the truth. The leaders of the *March for Jesus* think marching will restrain the powers of darkness. But the *March for Jesus* is lead by false teachers. Catholic participants believe in "co-redeemers", and "co-saviours". They pray to the dead. They believe they are going to purgatory for their sins, even though the blood of Jesus cleanses us from all sin.

Roger Forster teaches that we can not be sure there is an eternal hell. In the United States there is violence, crime, pornography on television, legalized abortion, Christian clergy saying not to believe in the virgin birth, and urging that we ordain homosexuals and lesbians. Islam openly claims to have an agenda from God to restore the moral fabric of this society and put an end to crime. They state that Judaism and Christianity are morally and spiritually bankrupt. Islam claims that it can do what Christianity has failed to do.

Some people think we can roll on the floor and laugh because God is doing a wonderful thing in our nation. That is the mentality of the Rodney Howard-Brownes and John Kilpatricks of this world. The question is: which god? Others are saying: "bind and loose", "speak dominion", "go forth in power marches". They can claim all they want. It is New Age, Islam, homosexuality, crime, witchcraft and tribal religions that are going on in power, not the church. We need a march of repentance and genuine salvation. The blood of Christ Jesus redeems from all sin. Go forth in the power of the cross. Repent and be saved. Without proper theology, there will be no doxology.

And knowing their thoughts He said to them, "Any kingdom divided against itself is laid waste; and any city or house divided against itself shall not stand. And if Satan casts out Satan, he is divided against himself; how shall his kingdom stand? And if by Beelzebub I cast out demons, by whom do your sons cast them out? Consequently they shall be your judges. But if I cast out demons by the Spirit of God, then the kingdom of God has come upon you. Or how can anyone enter the strong man's house and carry off his property unless he first binds the strong man? And then he will plunder his house. He who is not with Me is against Me; and He who does not gather with Me scatters" (Matthew 12:25-32).

In the temptation of Christ recorded in Matthew 4:1-11, Satan twisted scripture out of context. In Genesis 3:1-7 he did the same with Eve, creating doubts. "Hath God said?" Satan did it with Eve, did it with Adam, and even tried to do it with Jesus.

How did Jesus respond? The whole argument between Satan and Jesus came from the book of Deuteronomy. Satan quoted from Deuteronomy out of context, and Jesus quoted from Deuteronomy in context "It is written..." "That's right, but it is also written..."

Satan laughs at Christians who seek to use Matthew 12:29 out of context.

What is the context of "binding the strong man"—Matthew 12:29? The context tells us that the Pharisees accused Jesus of casting out demons by the power of Satan: the context is exorcism, casting out demons. This is the closest we come in the New Testament to a description of the sin of blaspheming the Holy Spirit: not a definition, but an illustration of it. The religious leaders were attributing to Satan that which they knew was of God in order to keep themselves in positions of power, for their own financial and social advantage. They knowingly misused their position to turn people against the truth. The same thing is occurring today where religious leaders are turning others away from the truth. This happens, for example, when they tell people: "Don't read *Christianity in Crisis* by Hank Hanegraaf," knowing that book tells the truth.

In cases of real demon possession, a person cannot be saved until you first cast out the demons. The New Testament will help you determine and discern biblically whether it is an authentic demon or not. If you do exercise the discernment of spirits, it will always be with the bible as your guideline. Demon possession is accompanied by irrational behaviour. People throwing themselves into the fire, gashing themselves, living in tombs, displaying superhuman strength or superhuman intelligence, counterfeiting the gifts of the spirit. Signs and wonders can be displayed by demons. Another sign is the presence of a physical malady without any pathology for it (ie, a physical ailment with no medical reason for it).

Read Dr Kurt Koch. Read good books on the subject. In cases of demon possession, the person's spirit is inhabited by an evil spirit. The Holy Spirit cannot enter them until the demon is cast out. You cannot set a demon possessed person free merely by witnessing to them.

And Jesus answered and said to him, "Blessed are you, Simon Bar Jona, because flesh and blood did not reveal this to you, but My Father who is in heaven. And I also say to you that you are Peter, and upon this rock I will build My church; and the gates of Hades shall not over power it.

"I will give you the keys of the kingdom of heaven; and whatever you shall bind on earth shall be bound in heaven, and whatever you shall loose on earth shall be loosed in heaven." Then He warned the disciples that they should tell no one that He was the Christ (Matthew 16:17).

These verses are used as the basis for Roman Catholic heresy that Peter was the first Pope, that Peter was *the rock*. The Pope claims he can do whatever he wants because he has the keys. Whatever he binds is bound, and whatever he looses is loosed. But 'Peter' means *pebble* in Greek. The 'rock' is Christ.

For I do not want you to be unaware, brethren, that our fathers were all under the cloud, and all passed through the sea; and all were baptized into Moses in the cloud and in the sea; and all ate the same spiritual food; and all drank the same spiritual drink, for they were drinking from a spiritual rock which followed them; and the rock was Christ (1 Corinthians 10:1-4).

None of the early church fathers ever said that Peter was *the rock*. They all say that Christ was *the rock*. Galatians 2:11 records the fact that Paul opposed Peter to his face because of his hypocrisy. What? Paul rebuked the Pope? It is absurd.

Who presided over the first church council at Jerusalem, recorded in Acts 15? Was it Peter? No, it was James. He convened the first council, not Peter. The Catholics have no biblical or historical evidence for their doctrine. If Peter was the first bishop of Rome, how come it was Paul that wrote the epistle to Romans, not Peter? Peter's ministry was primarily to the Jews (Galatians 2:7).

Giving these keys has nothing to do with 'Papal authority'. This is ridiculous.

There have been rival popes at certain times. Whichever family had the money, power and the better army—they prevailed.

They hurled anathemas and curses at one another, and the less powerful popes came to be called 'Antichrist'. Clement XIV (1769-74) abolished "forever" the Jesuits. Pius XII (1800-20) restored the Jesuits; one "infallible" Pope restoring for all time what another "infallible" pope just before him had abolished forever!

And to the angel of the church in Philadelphia write: He who is holy, who is true, who has the key of David, who opens and no one will shut, and who shuts and no one opens, says this: know your deeds. Behold, I have put before you an open door which no one can shut, because you have a little power, and have kept My word, and have not denied My name. Behold, I will cause those of the synagogue of Satan, who say that they are Jews, and are not, but lie—behold, I will make them to come and bow down at your feet, and to know that I have loved you. Because you have kept the word of My perseverance, I also will keep you from the hour of testing, that hour which is about to come upon the whole world, to test those who dwell upon the earth. *I am coming quickly; hold fast what you have, in order that no one take your crown* (Revelation 3:7–11).

Philadelphia was a good church, with little power; not like the big churches today which are run by world-famous, rich, influential men, who are all after more power. The Lord Jesus Christ put before the church at Philadelphia an open door which no one can shut, because they had little power. These were faithful Christians making up one of the best churches; it was not a flaky church. He told them, "You have no power; I have to open the door for you." Jesus has those keys. He never gave those keys to anyone. With those keys He opens and He closes.

And when I saw Him, I fell at His feet as a dead man. And He laid His right hand upon me, saying, "Do not be afraid; I am the first and the last, and the living One; and I was dead, and behold, I am alive for evermore, and I have the keys of death and of Hades.

"Write therefore the things which you have seen, and the things which are, and the things which shall take place after these things. As for the mystery of the seven stars which you saw in My right hand and the seven golden lampstands: the seven stars are the angels of the seven churches, and the seven lampstands are the seven churches" (Revelation 1:17–20).

"The living One... has... the keys of death and Hades" (Revelation 1:18). Jesus has the keys to death and Hades. Jesus has the power to say who goes to hell and who does not. The Pope claims that he has the keys; he does not. Only Christ Jesus has the keys for that.

Woe to you lawyers! For you have taken away the key of knowledge; you did not enter in yourselves, and those who were entering in you hindered (Luke 11:52). The Pharisees were misusing their knowledge of the scriptures to create a power base for themselves politically and financially. They were holding the power of death and hell over people, much like the popes of the middle ages.

"How dare you speak against them! You will go to hell for speaking against them. They will pronounce judgment on you !" Today it is not just popes that do that, hyper-pentecostals are doing the same.

The spirit of antichrist is a man putting himself in the place of God. One of the most dangerous antichrist spirits in the world today is not in catholicism, it is in Kingdom Now theology. The Greek term *antichrist* does not mean 'against Christ', it means 'in place of,' one who acts vicariously for Christ. In English, one who acts vicariously—in the place of another—is termed a 'vicar'. The true vicar of Christ is the Spirit of the Most High God, the Spirit of Truth, the Comforter (John 14:15-17; 16:7-11). He acts in the place of Jesus.

When you put someone in the place of the Holy Spirit and say that he is the 'vicar of Christ', he becomes antichrist, a counterfeit of the Holy Spirit. The papal title 'Vicar of Christ' is translated in Greek as *antichristos*. Every pope who puts on that title is saying, "I am Antichrist". The Holy Spirit is the true vicar of Christ.

But this is not just a catholic phenomenon. Earl Paulk from the United States communicates with the dead. He says, "I know what the bible teaches about witchcraft, seances, and familiar spirits, but for every counterfeit, there is a real."

Note: Paulk begins with the counterfeit, not the real. The Word of God is true. Let's begin with the real. Whatever does not agree with the Word of God is the counterfeit. We know that in scripture we have that which is real.

Men like Earl Paulk, Kenneth Copeland, Rodney Howard-Browne use the counterfeit to try to find what is real. They talk to the dead as to the "cloud of witnesses", taking that verse out of context to mean that you can talk to the dead. This is an abomination to God. The Catholics talk to dead saints and familiar spirits. When King Saul called up evil spirits and talked to the dead (1 Samuel 28:7-19), it was an abomination. Saul was judged unto destruction for doing that.

People who claim to get revelation knowledge from dead people, as Earl Paulk does, are committing abomination. When Benny Hinn gets the anointing from the bones of the dead bodies at the grave sites of Aimee Semple McPherson and Kathryn Kuhlman, he is committing abomination.

Every false religion in the world says: "the Bible AND something else". The Catholic church, the Mormon church, the Jehovah witnesses organisation, they all say the Word of God AND tradition, the Word of God AND the inventions of men. What did Jesus say about the inventions of men? He condemned them. It is the Word of God and nothing else! The Pharisees were condemned for "teaching as doctrines the precepts of men" (Matthew 15:9).

Satan tried to Judaize the church before he paganized it. The eastern orthodox and catholic religions paganized everything by Judaizing them first, putting people back under the law.

Earl Paulk says it is the voice of older prophets speaking to him with the words of God, and therefore it is God speaking to him. These false teachers and prophets say it is Antichrist who is coming against *them* Oral Roberts, Earl Paulk, and Kenneth Copeland—who says he could have died on the cross instead of Jesus Christ—if you speak against their false teaching they say that you are of the spirit of antichrist.

They say it is God speaking; not them. Morris Cerullo says when you look at him, you are not looking at a man, you are looking at Jesus Christ.

We know that, when He appears, we shall be like Him (1 John 3:2). *Christ in you, the hope of glory* (Colossians 1:27). Yes, but, "We are Christs"? No! That is the spirit of antichrist. It began in catholicism, but today it is in hyper-pentecostalism and hyper-charismaticism. There are many antichrists. Anyone who puts them self in the place of Christ is antichrist. There is only one true vicar of Christ, and that is the Holy Spirit. And there is only one true basis of authority—God's Holy Word.

What these religious lawyers try to do is to use this authority for themselves—defining doctrine so as to secure their social, financial and political power base. Roman Catholicism has always done this.

"But woe to you, scribes and Pharisees, hypocrites, because you shut off the kingdom of heaven from men; for you do not enter in yourselves, nor do you allow those who are entering to go in... Even so you too outwardly appear righteous to men, but inwardly you are full of hypocrisy and lawlessness" (Matthew 23:13,28).

"Listen to another parable. There was a landowner who planted a vineyard and put a wall around it and dug a winepress in it, and built a tower, and rented it out to vine-growers, and went on a journey.

"And when the harvest time approached, he sent his slaves to the vinegrowers to receive his produce. And the vine-growers took his slaves and beat one, and killed another, and stoned a third. Again he sent another group larger than the first; and they did the same thing to them.

"But afterward he sent his son to them, saying, 'They will respect my son.'
"But when the vine-growers saw the son, they said among themselves, 'This is the heir; come, let us kill him, and seize his inheritance.' And they took him, and threw him out of the vineyard, and killed him. Therefore when the owner of the vineyard comes, what will he do to those vine-growers?"

They said to Him, "He will bring those wretches to a wretched end, and will rent out the vineyard to other vine-growers, who will pay him the proceeds at the proper seasons."

Jesus said to them, "Did you never read in the scriptures, 'The stone which the builders rejected, this became the chief cornerstone; this came about from the Lord, and it is marvellous in our eyes'? Therefore I say to you, the kingdom of God will be taken away from you, and be given to a nation producing the fruit of it. And he who falls on this stone shall be broken to pieces; but on whomever it falls, it will scatter him like dust." And when the chief priests and the Pharisees heard His parables, they understood that He was speaking about them (Matthew 21:37-45).

Jesus has promised that the people who use the vineyard for their own selfish purposes will lose all claim to it.

And after they had stopped speaking, James answered, saying, "Simeon has related how God first concerned Himself about taking from among the Gentiles a people for his name. And with this the words of the Prophets agree, just as it is written ... [and he quotes from Amos 9:11-12] *Therefore it is my judgment that...* (Acts 15:13-15,19).

It was James speaking, not Peter, so how did the catholic church come up with their story that Peter was the leader? This is why the catholic church put the bible on their *Index of Forbidden Books*.

Then it seemed good to the apostles and the elders, with the whole church, to choose men from among them to send to Antioch with Paul and Barnabas... and they sent this letter by them, "The apostles and the brethren who are elders, to the brethren in Antioch, Syria, and Cilicia who are from the Gentiles..." (Acts 15:22-23).

The Greek word for 'bind' is *'dao'* ; the equivalent of the Hebrew word *'hitir'* meaning 'allowed'. The Greek word for 'loose' is *'luo'*; the equivalent of the Hebrew word *'asur'* meaning 'forbidden '. These are juridical terms still used in Jewish law called *'haleka'*.

Non-Jews accepting Christ were "loosed" from Mosaic law, but still "bound" to refrain from blood, idolatry, strangulation, and immorality, which derived from God's commands to Noah called 'Noahide law'.

The apostolic brethren spoke corporately. Jesus gave the keys of knowledge to the apostles so that they would know what the scriptures meant. Acts chapter 15 is apostolic binding and loosing in action; the apostles used those keys to interpret Amos 9:11-12. Acts 15 clearly describes the use of the keys.

What did they bind? "Keep these four commandments."

What did they loose? The Law of Moses from the people, as the Messiah has fulfilled the law. They defined doctrine. They explained: "This is what Jeremiah meant; this is what Amos meant".

Now we have the keys of knowledge, we understand the scriptures. The rabbis have rejected their Messiah and are going into error. But we have the authority, we bind and we loose. The apostles did not use that authority for heavy shepherding, they used it for correcting wrong doctrine.

Apostolic authority is always about doctrine—Galatians, Corinthians, Thessalonians. It was always used for correcting wrong doctrine. They had the keys of authority and knowledge. Apostolic authority was always plural and it was always about doctrine.

And if your brother sins, go and reprove him in private; if he listens to you, you have won your brother But if he does not listen to you, take one or two more with you, so that by the mouth of two or three witnesses every fact may be confirmed. And if he refuses to listen to them, tell it to the church; and if he refuses to listen even to the church, let him be to you as a Gentile and a tax gatherer. Truly I say unto you, whatever you shall bind on earth shall be bound in heaven; and whatever you shall loose on earth shall be loosed in heaven. Again I say to you, that if two of you agree on earth about anything that they may ask, it shall be done for them by My Father who is in heaven. For where two or three have gathered together in My name, there I am in their midst (Matthew 18:15-20).

Look at the context. This is about going to a brother about sin, not doctrine. If someone refuses to repent of their sin, you can bind and loose. What does that mean, and how did the apostles apply it? Not the way people are applying it today. We read the teachings of Jesus and the rest of the bible through the prism of the teachings of the apostles. Think of the epistles as inspired commentary, God's commentary. The epistles are the prism of the apostles. They tell you in a clear and practical way what the rest of the bible means, what the teaching of Jesus means.

It is actually reported that there is immorality among you, and immorality of such a kind as does not exist even among the Gentiles, that someone has his father's wife. And you have become arrogant, and have not mourned instead, in order that the one who had done this deed might be removed from your midst (1 Corinthians 5:1-2).

So many leaders today would disagree with Paul's attitude. "Now don't judge our doctrine". A lot of leaders would say, "You are judging, leave our doctrine alone."

For on my part [ie, as an apostle], *though absent in body but present in spirit, have already judged him who has so committed this, as though I were present. In the name of our Lord Jesus, when you are assembled, and I with you in spirit, with the power of our Lord Jesus, I have decided to deliver such a one to Satan for the destruction of his flesh, that his spirit may be saved in the day of the Lord Jesus* (1 Corinthians 5:3-5).

Paul used his authority to give this person over to Satan for the destruction of his flesh. He used his authority and bound a wayward believer. What is the context of the reference to binding and loosing in. Matthew 18? When the person would not repent of their sin, the church had the authority to agree to put this person under a judgment; they could bind him, tie him up—not with the view of seeing him destroyed, but with the view of seeing him restored. Look at the context: they were pronouncing judgment on a soul for his restoration.

We have looked at the two times Jesus used the term "bind" (Greek *deo*) and it does not have anything whatsoever to do with what so many preachers are telling you to do today. Apostolic authority exists to define doctrine and to deal with persistent immorality and perverse sin in the Body.

For the married woman is bound by law to her husband while he is living, but if her husband dies, she is released from the law concerning the husband. So then if, while her husband is living, she is joined to another man, she shall be called an adulteress, but if her husband dies, she is free from the law, though she is joined to another man (Romans 7:2-3).

All mankind is under the law of sin and death, of which the Mosaic law is a symbol. Understand what the law of Moses meant. The Jews are more accountable because they had it written down. The Jews had the oracles of God and salvation was available to them first, and the responsibility was on them first.

I have a balloon here. If I let go of it, the law of gravity says the balloon will fall down. But if I pump helium in the balloon before I release it, the law of buoyancy will make the balloon go up and not fall. The law of buoyancy is a stronger law than the law of gravity; it will supersede the law of gravity.

The law of Moses teaches that we have a fallen nature. There is nothing wrong with the law. It teaches that we need a Messiah; we need a stronger law to keep us from falling. Unsaved people have no choice, they must sin. Believers are not under the law, we do not have to sin. We are under the power of the Holy Spirit.

Christians do sin, but they have a choice that unsaved people do not have. We have buoyancy, we have helium. We do not have to sin, because we have the Holy Spirit. Therefore, like the Jews, we are more responsible for our sin than the unsaved person. The law is our tutor. It teaches the need for a Messiah to save us. The purpose of the law is to show us we cannot keep the law. The gospel looses, forgives; setting people free from the law of sin and death. The gospel frees.

If you forgive the sins of any their sins have been forgiven them; and if you retain the sins of any they have been retained (John 20:23).

The idea that, by these words, Jesus introduced the Roman Catholic sacrament of 'penance' is absurd. There is no such thing as 'penance' in the bible, nor any record of it being practised by the early church fathers. Telling your sins to the priests was a Babylonian custom. In the early church there was no 'penance', but there was repentance. As Luther learned from the French humanist scholar Lefèvre, the Greek word means 'repent', not 'penance'; Rome lied.

People would ask each other for forgiveness for a wrong done, but they never went to a "priest" for this. Those things all came later. They are human inventions, created for the same reason as the Pharisees' teachings: *money and power*, the same reason the hyper-charismatic churches are inventing doctrines today: *money and power*.

And He was teaching in one of the synagogues on the Sabbath. And behold, there was a woman who for eighteen years had a sickness caused by a spirit; and she was bent double, and could not straighten up at all.

And when Jesus saw her, He called her over and said to her, "Woman, you are freed from your sickness." And He laid His hands upon her; and immediately she was made erect again, and began glorifying God. And the synagogue official became indignant because Jesus had healed on the Sabbath, began saying to the multitude in response, "There are six days in which work should be done; therefore come during them and get healed, and not on the Sabbath day." But the Lord answered him and said, "You hypocrites, does not each of you on the Sabbath untie his ox or his donkey from the stall, and lead him away to water him? And this woman, a daughter of Abraham as she is, whom Satan has bound for eighteen long years, should she not have been released from this bond on the Sabbath day?" And as He said this, all His opponents were being humiliated; and the entire multitude was rejoicing over all the glorious things being done by Him (Luke 13:10-17).

Demonic oppression can bind people. This woman was not demon possessed, she suffered from demonic oppression. That can make people sick. Yes, there are gifts of healing. Yes, we can anoint the sick. Yes, we can pray. And yes, we can do what Jesus did. He laid his hands on her and immediately she was freed. No one says we cannot loose in this situation. But Jesus never did anything except what He saw His Father do.

And it came about one day that He was teaching; and there were some Pharisees and teachers of the law sitting there, who had come from every village of Galilee and Judea and from Jerusalem; and the power of the Lord, was present for Him to perform healing (Luke 5:17).

We can pray for healing and anoint with oil. If somebody has sickness, caused by sin (as in James 5:14-15 and in Psalm 32:3-5), if that person repents, the sickness will leave because it is the consequence of sin. We can pray for the sick, but, if you are going to tell people to get out of their wheelchair or get out of their coffin, the *dunamis* (Greek, "power") had better be there, as it was for Jesus. The Holy Spirit had better be leading you to tell that person to do what you are saying. If the Holy Spirit is leading, it will happen; but if the Spirit is not leading, it will not happen.

Jesus only did what He saw His Father doing.

Paul prayed three times for freedom from demonic oppression (2 Corinthians 12:7-9). God said no. "My grace is sufficient for you, for power is perfected in weakness." God said he would leave Paul under this for His own purposes. You can only do what the Lord tells you to do. He will never allow us to experience more temptation or problems than we can handle.

No temptation has overtaken you but such as is common to man; and God is faithful who will not allow you to be tempted beyond what you are able, but with the temptation will provide the way of escape also, that you may be able to endure it (1 Corinthians 10:13).

You can pray, repent and be saved. If you truly believe in your heart, you will be saved. His grace will be there; certain things will always be there for us. But some things are not provided in every situation. It is how God leads in the situation. We cannot bind and loose every circumstance as we see fit.

He who had died came forth, bound hand and foot with wrappings; and his face was wrapped around with a cloth. Jesus said to them, "Unbind him, and let him go" (John 11:44).

This is a perfect picture of what happens in salvation. When I was in Israel, at Bethany, where Lazarus was buried, the Lord showed this to me. It turns out that I was not as spiritual as I thought, because George Whitefield was shown the same thing some two hundred years earlier by the Lord. *"Remove the stone... Lazarus, come forth... Unbind him, and let him go"* (John 11:39 ,43,44).

This is midrash. When we witness to an unsaved person, the only thing we are doing is rolling away the stone. We are making it possible for them to hear the voice of Jesus. You can witness until you are blue in the face, but until they hear the voice of Jesus, it is useless. When we witness, the only thing we are doing is rolling away the stone.

I am the good shepherd; and I know My own, and My own know Me, even as the Father knows Me and I know the Father; and I lay down My life for the sheep.

My sheep hear My voice, and I know them, and they follow Me, and I give eternal life to them, and they shall never perish, and no one shall snatch them out of My hand. My Father, who has given them to Me, is greater than all; and no one is able to snatch them out of the Father's hand. I and the Father are one (John 10:14-15, 27).

All we can do is roll away the stone; tell the unsaved, and pray. But that is it. There comes a time when you have done all you can. You can be a witness to them and an example, and be available. Then it is up to God. Sometimes there will be calamity in their lives which causes them to reconsider the gospel. But only the Son of Man can call that which is dead unto life.

Truly, truly, I say to you, he who hears My word, and believes Him who sent Me, has eternal life, and does not come into judgment, but has passed out of death into life. Truly, truly, I say to you, an hour is coming and now is, when the dead shall hear the voice of the Son of God; and those who hear shall live. For just as the Father has life in Himself, even so He gave to the Son also to have life in Himself

(John 5:24-26).

If you are not born again, you are already dead spiritually. Your body is working, but you are already dead. Jesus wants to call you from death unto life. He wants to forgive your sins and give you eternal life.

Your body may be alive but you are already dead. Only the Son of Man can call that which is dead unto life. "Lazarus come forth." But when Lazarus came out, Jesus said "You unbind him."

What is it that we loose? Discipleship, baptism, counselling. Do you understand? YOU unbind him.

This is the "fellowship of the saints". We all come into the kingdom of God with baggage from the world. When people become Christians, they arrive spiritually oppressed, emotionally bound, with all kinds of problems. They need discipleship.

There are biblical and unbiblical versions of 'binding and loosing'. As you see, none of it has anything to do with what most Pentecostal churches are teaching today.

The preaching of the gospel will always come first. (Paul preached the gospel.) Prayer and fasting come next. (What did Esther and Daniel do?) And third comes intercession and prayer for those in authority, for the political leaders who have authority over God's people.

First of all, then, I urge that entreaties and prayers, petitions and thanksgivings, be made on behalf of all men for kings and all who are in authority in order that we may lead a tranquil and quiet life in all godliness and dignity. This is good and acceptable in the sight of God our Saviour, who desires all men to come to the knowledge of the truth (1 Timothy 2:1-4).

You may not like politics or politicians, but if they are not influenced by our prayers, they will be influenced by something else. When did the Third Reich happen in Germany? When evangelical Christianity declined and 'higher criticism' had replaced it. What did the Germans do? They became genocidal exterminators, butchers of whole civilizations. The Germans went back and did the same things that they had done in their pre-Christian times. The gospel stopped being preached. The church compromised. Then the government came under the influence of wickedness.

Now in England they are starting to hold pagan festivals again. Where? Stonehenge, Glastonbury, the same places where the druids, wicca (Anglo-saxon witchcraft) and the pre-Christian Britons did. When? At the summer solstice, the vernal equinox. It does not matter what they are called, they are druid high priests. It is the same things occurring in the same places. When the preaching of the gospel becomes compromised with false leaders (such as George Carey), the ancient territorial spirits, if you want to use the term, resurface. The government comes under the influence of wickedness and godlessness. Outside the English parliament it says, "Our Father Who art in Heaven". On the inside there are Moslems, atheists, Freemasons, and God-only-knows what else, voting on the appointment of Anglican bishops. In Japan, the philosophy of the corporations is based on the old shogun model of the shinto religion. It has always been around.

First, the preaching of the gospel. Second, prayer and fasting and intercession of God's people, especially for those in government. God ordained human government to hold back evil, and if it is not being influenced by our prayers it will certainly become an instrument for evil itself. The early Christians even prayed for the Roman emperors, so that the gospel could prosper under their rule. When will the Antichrist be openly manifested? When the lordship of history is given into the hand of Satan for a fixed period of three and one half years.

And you know what restrains him now, so that in his time he may be revealed. For the mystery of lawlessness is already at work; only he who now restrains will do so until he is taken out of the way. And then that lawless one will be revealed whom the Lord will slay with the breath of His mouth and bring to an end by the appearance of His coming that is, the one whose activity is in accord with the activity of Satan, with all power and signs and false wonders, and with all the deception of wickedness for those who perish, because they did not receive the love of the truth so as to be saved.

And for this reason God will send upon them a deluding influence so that they might believe what is false, in order that they all may be judged who did not believe the truth, but took pleasure in wickedness (2 Thessalonians 2:6-12).

The spirit of Antichrist is already here. But He who restrains will do so until He is taken out of the way. The Holy Spirit will not always function in the way He does now. Grace will come to an end. We need to be careful about taking dispensationalism too far, but the age of grace will come to an end. In the Book of Revelation, God goes back to dealing with man the way he did in the Old Testament; judgment, wrath, grace comes to an end. The power of the Holy Spirit to convict the unsaved and to empower the church to preach the gospel will come to an end.

The great tribulation, with the Holy Spirit being withdrawn from the world and the church being raptured, are not synonymous; they are separate, but related events.

But once the Holy Spirit is grieved by sin in the church, once the light becomes dim and the salt looses its taste, what are we going to have? The resurgence of wickedness.

It is the convicting power of the Holy Spirit that makes the church age possible. Once He is grieved and withdraws, the innate evil of the world system will quickly re-emerge.

If you love Me, you will keep my commandments. And I will ask the Father, and He will give you another Helper, that He may be with you forever that is the Spirit of truth... (John 14:15-17).

But I tell you the truth, it is to your advantage that I go a way, for if I do not go away, the Helper shall not come to you; but if I go, I will send Him to you. And He, when He comes, will convict the world concerning sin, and righteousness, and judgment,—concerning sin, because they do not believe in Me; and concerning righteousness, because I go to the Father, and you no longer behold Me; and concerning judgment, because the ruler of this world has been judged. These things I have spoken to you, that in Me you may have peace. In the world you have tribulation, but take courage,—I have overcome the world (John 16:7-11,33).

It is the prayers and fasting of God's people for those in government, and the preaching of the gospel that restrains wickedness.

These three are the only things that will restrain wickedness in the world today:

1) preaching of the gospel; in Ephesians 6 we put on the shoes and pick up the sword;

2) prayer and fasting, especially prayer for government leaders;

3) the convicting power of the Holy Spirit.

These are the correct ways to use the instruments of binding and loosing. If you want to get somewhere, use the correct instrument—put down the fork and pick up the spoon.

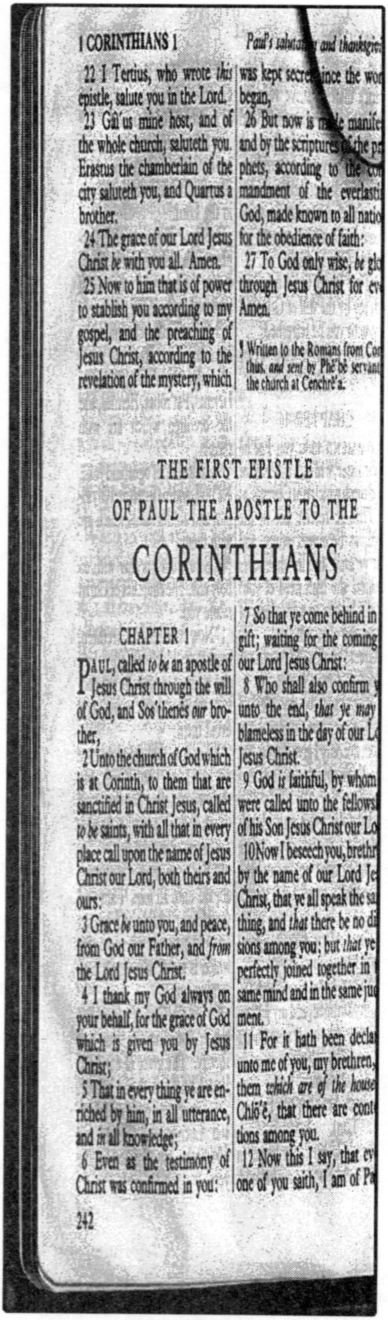
1 CORINTHIANS 1
THE FIRST EPISTLE
OF PAUL THE APOSTLE TO THE
CORINTHIANS
CHAPTER 1
242

BIBLE VERSIONS

I CANNOT tell you how many times people have come to me with a copy of a book such as Gail Riplinger's *New Age Bible Versions,* very confused about which bible version to read, and asking questions like:

- "Is it true that only the King James Version follows the original Greek and Hebrew texts?"
- "Is it true that all the other texts have been mutilated in some way?"
- "Do you know that New Agers say *The Christ*?"
- "Do you know there was a lesbian on the translation committee of the N.I.V.?"

Now, is there any basis for all this stuff? Let's begin at the beginning.

During December 1996, I went into hospital for tests on my neck. I consulted one of the most highly respected neuro-radiologists in Africa—a British educated, Jewish woman who came to faith through our ministry in South Africa, Dr Hilda Podlas, an expert in neuro-radiology (she writes for medical journals and lectures on the subject). And in Britain I had a Magnetic Resonance Imaging scan on my neck. All the neuro-surgeons and neurologists, consulting together, came to the same conclusion: *We could operate on your neck, but there is not a sufficiently high enough probability that surgery would either reduce the pain or prevent future degeneration. If there was any reasonable chance of either or both those outcomes we would recommend surgery, but as things are we cannot make that recommendation.*

I went to see the best specialists in South Africa and Britain, and all the experts agreed. No problem. Incidentally, I had those medical tests thanks to my membership of a health insurance fund. How I came to have that health insurance is an interesting story.

When I was in bible college, my church in London had a new heat pump installed in the basement of the building. But it was not implemented correctly. One dark, rainy night, when I was leaving the building, I noticed boiling water pouring off the main roof onto a lower roof. I did not know what it was, but I was afraid that it might cause an electrical fire. So I decided to investigate—not by going back inside and up the stairs to look out a window with a torch to see what it was, but by climbing up on the spike-topped cast iron railing that surrounded the old building. The railing was wet. My foot slipped. And one of the spikes went through my ribs and into my chest, driving my pectoral muscle into my lung.

I was impaled and there was no one around. That was only the beginning of calamities. Getting off the spike was the second. And the third was that the British National Health Service was in such a bad way that the hospital staff asked me to "be a good Christian" and sign myself out of hospital while I was still in need of treatment. They promised that they would send visiting nurses around to repack my chest. We had no money for private health insurance (I was a seminary student at the time) and I wanted to "be a good Christian", so I signed myself out of hospital. Then my chest became infected and I almost failed my last year of bible college. So I said, "I can live like this, but God forbid that it should happen to my wife and children." And although it cost us a lot of money, by our standards at the time, we have had health insurance ever since.

I went into hospital last December to have the tests on my neck. But somebody goofed up. I was supposed to have a Magnetic Resonance

Imaging (MRI) scan, but they had me down for a cerebral angiogram. Some clerk not trained in medical terminology goofed the thing up. Thanks to my medical training, I knew the difference and was able to redirect the hospital staff.

I spotted the mistake in time and everything turned out alright. But what would have happened if I did not have that medical knowledge? Anyone who did not know what a cerebral angiogram was would have had the wrong test. Here we have two cases. In one case we have expert medical opinion all agreed. In the other case we have an untrained clerk arranging for someone to undergo the wrong procedure.

The debate about bible versions is no different. There is a divide between scholarly people who can read Hebrew and Greek, who have studied theology and biblical archaeology and textual criticism all their lives, and a group of vocal individuals who do not have the scholarship background to be making the claims they do.

Gail Riplinger seems impressive. She has letters after her name "B.A.", "M.A." and "M.F.A." from Cornell University and Harvard University. Very impressive. What she doesn't tell you is that her degrees are in "Home Economics"! Gail Riplinger has no relevant theological or language qualifications at all.

Last week I visited my dentist to have a cap put on a tooth. My dentist is Maurice Green, a Jewish guy who prayed with me to receive the Lord many years ago. His son was the vice principal of London Bible College and the chairman of *Jews for Jesus* in the U.K. Maurice is a very good dentist. I also visited a lawyer last week. The barrister is Rex Makin, who is considered to be the best litigation attorney in the north of England. Good for Rex Makin, but he is not going to cap my teeth. Maurice Green is an excellent dentist, but I do not want him to represent me in a court of law.

What happens when an average person, not trained in Hebrew and Greek, reads a book like Riplinger's *New Age Bible Versions,* a book produced by someone not qualified to write on the subject?

If you are going to pontificate on bible versions you should have been to seminary. At the very least you should have done basic studies in theology. You should have studied Hebrew and Greek, and completed some university-level studies in textual criticism. You should have a better than passing acquaintance with biblical archaeology—you should understand how we came to have the various manuscripts that we do today.

Gail Riplinger was interviewed by Wayne House, a conservative, evangelical Christian scholar. Wayne House reports that she "repeatedly mispronounced terms used by biblical scholars"[1]. After he had asked her four times, "she hesitatingly admitted that she could not read Greek."[2]

It is not a simple matter to reach an informed opinion regarding biblical texts and correct translations. When I consulted the experts regarding my neck, there were three neural radiologists, two neurosurgeons and four neurologists, all looking at the same MRI scans. Each of them expressed their personal opinion. They were not looking to make a political decision, they were looking for a right decision. They were considering a technical problem, with each bringing their own technical perspective and professional experience to bear on the question. Medicine is not an exact science. There is always a margin of discrepancy.

The same applies to textual criticism. It is not as easy as people make it out to be. With Gail Riplinger we have someone who does not know what she is doing, causing enormous upset in the lives of untrained Christians.

Wayne House points that the only good thing about Riplinger's book is that it "is not any longer than it is and that the foolishness of its various claims are transparent when one takes the time to study them"[3]. I have to agree with him. *New Age Bible Versions* is rubbish, absolute rubbish. This is not to put down the King James Version, and it is not to endorse other versions.

Personally, I do not think the New International Version (NIV) is a good translation. It is structured on a thought-by-thought basis, rather than a word-by-word basis. Whenever you take that approach to translation work, you end up with too much of the translator's personal interpretation.

All translations carry a certain amount of interpretation. If you had a speaker in one language with three fluent speakers of that language translating into another language in which they were also fluent, the three translations would differ in many ways. There is always a subjective element in translation work.

The Greek of the New Testament *(koine)* is trying to convey Hebraic or Aramaic thoughts to a Hellenistic world. Which is not to say that you need to be a Greek or Hebrew scholar to understand the bible. You do not. But if you are going to make definitive pronouncements—this is the right one and that is the wrong one—you had better know what you are talking about. Some of the conclusions that Gail Riplinger has arrived at are absolutely absurd.

There is such a thing as acrostic algebra in the bible; see Psalm 119, for example. Many English translations insert headings—aleph, beth, gimel, daleth, etc.—above the relevant sections. And there is also such a thing as biblical numerics and numerical typology—twelve apostles, twelve tribes of Israel, one hundred and forty-four, multiples of four and seven, and so on. Certain numbers are associated with certain things.

There have been people like Ivan Panin (1855-1942)—a Russian who spent many years in the United States—who developed a system of numerical analysis late last century and early this century. His system is still being debated.

But Gail Riplinger teaches an absurd form of alphabetical algebra, where she subtracts the letters of carefully selected abbreviations from one another in order to end up with the letters SIN, which is supposed to show God's disapproval of translations other than the King James Version.

Wayne House conducted a parallel exercise with the abbreviations for the Cunards Authorized (CA), King James II (KJ2), Hayman's Epistles (HE), Revised English Bible (REB), New International Version (NIV), New American Standard Bible (NASB) and Barclays New Testament (BNT), and came up with the letters C H R I S T. What does that prove?

In fact, if you reverse the last three letters of Gail Riplinger's first name and add the first letter of her surname you get the letters LIAR. What does that prove?

And if someone were to declare that God had told them to carry out this piece of alphabetical acrobatics—as Riplinger claims regarding her absurd exercise—what would that prove? The whole thing is insane.

In a newsletter, Riplinger effectively claims divine inspiration for her own book[2].

"Daily, during the six years needed for this investigation, the Lord miraculously brought the needed materials and resources—much like the ravens fed Elijah. Each discovery was not the result of effort on my part, but of the direct hand of God—so much so that I hesitated to even put my name on the book. Consequently, I used G.A.Riplinger—God as author and Riplinger as secretary."

If God wrote this book, I would like to know why He made so many mistakes. Doesn't He know Greek and Hebrew?

There are genuine problems with some translations that exist today. For example, the *New Inclusive Bible* is a censored, politically-correct translation that is heretical.

There is a legitimate problem, but it must be addressed in a legitimate way. There is a New Age infiltration of the church going on today. But it must be addressed responsibly, not irresponsibly. When real problems are publicly and irresponsibly addressed by people who cannot be taken seriously, the arguments for truth become discredited.

A lot of what is said in the name of creationism is neither theologically nor scientifically responsible. Plausible arguments are easily discredited when advanced by crazy people. Hence the battle against the teaching of secular evolution is often damaged by creationists.

When God needed somebody to defend the Messiahship of Jesus to the Jewish establishment, He got a Pharisee to do it. When He needed somebody to carry the gospel to the Greco-Roman world and write the epistles—taking Jewish thoughts and communicating them to people with a Greek world-view—He got somebody who knew how to do it. It is unfortunate that people try to do things that they are not called or equipped to do.

In page after page, Riplinger attacks people. She does not attack people's views or teaching, but rather she slanders them, usually by taking things they said out of the context in which they said it. And on that false or distorted basis, she tries to say they are this or that or the other.

In a court of law, the rules of jurisprudence prevent this method of argument; Riplinger's attacks would simply be thrown out. Neither would it stand up in academic theology. In a scholarly debate her methods would be torn to bits.

For example, she attacks Edwin Palmer, the executive secretary of the NIV committee. Rip linger accuses Palmer of denying that the Holy Spirit played a role in the conception, the "begetting," of Jesus and tries to link his views to Mormon theology[3].

She probably does not know it, but the Greek word is *monogenes,* which includes far more than the English word "beget".

Palmer made the statement[4]: "The Holy Spirit did not beget the Son"—in relation to the eternal begetting of the Son from the Father within the trinity. It had nothing to do with Mary's begetting of Jesus. Riplinger quotes Palmer—out of all context—then follows with another quote from the Mormon, Brigham Young, regarding the physical conception of Jesus through Mary.

Palmer[5] says directly, in another place in his book, that the "Holy Spirit was needed at the very start of Jesus' human life, at his incarnation. By the word incarnation we mean the act by which the second Person of the trinity, remaining God, 'became flesh and lived for a while among us' (John 1:14)."

Riplinger has taken one statement by Palmer out of context, in order to falsely accuse him of denying the Holy Spirit's involvement in Jesus' physical conception, when Palmer—in the same book—has explicitly stated that the Holy Spirit *was* involved.

Wayne House[6] comments that: "This is careless scholarship or confused theology at best, but it may be outright deception on her part to prove her ill-founded theory about the supposed heresies of the NIV." Riplinger's method of suggesting that Edwin Palmer is a heretic is identical to that used against Jesus. *"We heard Him say, 'I will destroy this temple made with hands, and in three days I will build another made without hands.'"* (Mark 14:58).

They took the things He said out of context, and out of the overall context of His teaching, and falsely accused Him. This is the method of Satan - *the accuser of the brethren* (Revelation 12:10).

I do not like the NIV, but I am not going to go around telling people that Edwin Palmer is like the Mormons, just because I disagree with him from a scholarly perspective. Our disagreement does not make the man a heretic.

Riplinger charges that the translators of the NIV use the term "the Christ" in the same way as New Age people do. It is true that when New Agers say "the Christ" they mean "the Christ within". They are not referring to Jesus of Nazareth, the Messiah, they are referring to a spiritualist concept from the gnostic idea of the *Cosmic Illumination of the Inner Self.*

However, the Hebrew Old Testament uses the term *Ha Mashiach* —the Messiah (or the Christ or the Anointed One), because there were many messiahs—many anointed ones. Every king, every prophet and every priest was an 'anointed one'. The use of the definite article was necessary to indicate the ultimate 'anointed one' who was to come. Jesus is apart from and above all the other 'anointed ones', and this fact is indicated by the use of the definite article. The *Ha Mashiach* of the Old Testament becomes the *ho christos*—the Christ—of the New Testament. There is no problem here, except that Gail Riplinger says there is a problem.

"Real references to Jesus as 'the Christ' are rare: however, new versions literally paint their pages with this pawn"[7].

Look at the facts. The phrase "the Christ" appears 19 times in the King James Version. It appears 48 times in the NIV. The Greek *ho christos* appears 59 times in the (so-called) Textus Receptus. If you take into account all the instances of *ho christos* in its other case forms, the total number of times "the Christ" appears in the various Greek texts is:

Textus Receptus (1551)   = *169*
Majority-Byzantine   = *166*
Nestle-Aland 26th Ed.   = *146*

Which is to say that, if we take Riplinger at her word, the manuscript on which the King James Version is based contains more "New Age" references than the manuscripts used in the modern versions.

a) Her argument is, itself, stupid.

b) If the term "the Christ" is proof of heretical tendencies, then the King James Version is far more heretical than the translations that she attacks.

The whole thing is absurd. Gail Riplinger is a charlatan and a fraud. I do not know how much money she has made out of her book, but I know the damage she has done to many Christians.

Riplinger's basic argument is that any biblical manuscript which does not agree with the King James Version is an "addition" to the Word of God. But what do you do if the "addition" appears in manuscripts that pre-date the documents that the King James Version draws upon? In that case we can argue that it is the King James that contains "additions," not the other way around.

There are many ancient biblical manuscripts. Some are better than others. We have over ten thousand significant fragments of the New Testament; the oldest of which dates from the second century.

By comparison, we have only 420 copies of the *Conquests of Julius Caesar,* which shows that God is watching over His word to perform it.

Until the late nineteenth century, most texts used by bible translators were constructed from a compilation of manuscripts that went back to the seventh century. Some were fourth century, but most were seventh century.

Since the end of the last century we have access to far more manuscripts than previously. Riplinger urges that we ignore these and stick to the ones used in the translation of King James Version.

The KJV translators used something known as the *Textus Receptus* (meaning 'the received text') for the New Testament. Riplinger attacks all the alternative manuscripts as unreliable. But the *Textus Receptus* comes from something known as the *Majority Text,* which is not a source document in its own right. The *Textus Receptus* draws on at least four other source manuscripts, with the dominant source being from the Byzantine text tradition. Another text, called the *Alexandrinus,* draws on the same source. The *Textus Receptus,* in common with other texts that the King-James Only people condemn—has the same source! How can you say that this is the only right one, the others follow bad source texts, when they actually have a common source text? It is an absurd argument, but the average person would not know that.

The *Textus Receptus* did not even exist as a literary unit until Erasmus in the 16th century. Even the academically more credible KJV advocates such as the *Trinitarian Bible Society,* disassociate themselves from Gail Riplinger.

Riplinger says that, under the influences of Origen at Alexandria, all the other texts were mutilated to point away from the deity of Christ. Origen was a heretic. I do not deny that for one second. He had crazy, gnostic ideas, he castrated himself. The guy was nuts. I am no fan of Origen. However, Origen also wrote something called the *Hexapla,* where he published the six Greek versions of the bible available in his time alongside one another, so that people could compare them. What we know about his life shows that Origen was not trying to push any one version. These people claim all the other versions were mutilated, except the (so-called) *Majority Text,* which came to be the *Textus Receptus* and what evolved from that. It is pure conjecture. There is no proof Origen ever did what they say. On the contrary, the *Hexapla* indicates that the exact opposite is more likely. It listed various (mainly bad and Ebionite) texts.

Then they say "There was a lesbian on the translation committee of the NIV". Who 'authorised' the Authorised Version? It was not God, but some say a homosexual paedophile king who sodomised little boys—King James I of England. Does that negate the validity of the translation? Perverse as someone's sexual orientation may be, it has nothing to do with the quality of their scholarship. If you want to proceed at that level, the first translation you need to get rid of is the King James.

What do you do with the fact that the King James Version deviates repeatedly from both the *Textus Receptus* and the Hebrew Masoretic, text?

What do you do when the *Textus Receptus* says one thing and the King James mis-translates it? Or the words do not appear in the *Textus Receptus* and the King James adds them? Or the words appear in the *Textus Receptus* and the King James leaves them out? And what about the words found in the *Textus Receptus* which do not appear in any Greek text?

According to the King-James-Only people, the only correct Old Testament text is the Masoretic. But when the New Testament quotes from the Old Testament, it usually does not follow the Masoretic Text, but the Septuagint. Does that make the New Testament heretical?

In this century we have seen the hand of God in the discovery of the Dead Sea Scrolls. The 22 percent of the scrolls published so far show there has been no mutation (changing) of the bible text over the centuries.

I would have to argue that any bible version which pre-dates the finding of the Dead Sea Scrolls is, for scholarly purposes, obsolete. Not because the scrolls tell a different story, but because they affirm the accuracy of the texts handed down to us.

While many people have come to faith through the preaching of the King James Version, I am convinced that the KJV translators would have produced a slightly different version if they had had access to the materials available today. Even more ludicrous than Riplinger is Peter Ruckman who argues heretically that the additions to the KJV in 1611AD are "further revelation". Such views are akin to the Jehovah's Witness defence of their "New World Translation" bible.

There are good translations and there are bad translations. The King James is a valid bible. The NIV, although I do not like it, is a valid bible. The New American Standard Bible is a valid bible.

The Message, the New World Translation, the Inclusive Bible, the Couples Bible, the New Jerusalem Bible are not good translations.

The bible is the Word of God in the Word of Man. That does not make it any less the Word of God, but neither does that make it any less the Word of Man.

The minor discrepancies in the source texts available to us do not affect the historicity of the relevant events—that God became a man in the person of Jesus, that He taught these things, that He went to the Cross and died for our sins, that He rose from the dead, that we should live this way accordingly, that this is our future, that certain things are going to happen.

None of these facts or doctrines are affected.

The Word of God is still true.

God is still watching over His Word to perform it.

There are no problems with our bible.

1. House, H.Wayne 1994, *A Summary Critique: New Age Bible Versions,* in Christian Research Journal, Fall 1994, Christian Research Institute International.
2. Ibid.
3. Riplinger, G.A. 1993, New Age *Bible Versions,* A.V. Publications, p.344.
4. Palmer, Edwin H. 1974, *The Person and Ministry of the Holy Spirit,* Baker Book House, Grand Rapids Michigan, p.83.
5. ibid, p.65.
6. House, H.Wayne 1994, *A Summary Critique: New Age Bible Versions,* in Christian Research Journal, Fall 1994, Christian Research Institute International.
7. Riplinger, G.A. 1993, New *Age Bible Versions,* A.V. Publications, p.318.

For more detailed information on the general subject of English translations of the bible, see:

Carson, D.A. 1979, *The King James Version Debate: A Plea for Realism,* Baker Book House, Grand Rapids.

Lewis, Jack P. 1981, *The English Bible: From KJV to NIV,* Baker Book House, Grand Rapids.

TYPOLOGY OF THE TEMPLE

S OMEONE asked me, "When is the temple going to be rebuilt?" There are archaeological excavations (that are officially secret) that have been carried on by the Department of Antiquities of Hebrew University for some years. Everybody knows about them; they are not really secret. There have even been Christians involved in it, like Dr Jim Flemming. Dr Asher Kauffman of Hebrew University has done archaeological explorations beneath the Temple Mount, with the view to rebuilding it and violated an *halachic prohibition* against going up there. He found some bit of *Halachah* (Rabbinic law) that says that you can go on the Temple Mount to rebuild it. He actually went up on the Temple Mount to take some measurements, with a view to rebuilding it.

There is a movement to rebuild the temple. I would be very surprised if it was not rebuilt eventually, but this is a complicated subject. To understand it, we have to begin at the beginning.

There are at least three main words in Hebrew for *tabernacle* or *temple*, and three main words in Greek. In Hebrew the words are *mishkan*, which means 'tabernacle' or 'dwelling place,' *beit*, which means 'house,' and *haikhol* 'a temple'. The first Greek word is *oikos*, which simply means 'house.' The second is *naos*, which means 'shrine.' The third is *hieron*, which means 'temple.' They are used in different contexts, in different verses in the New Testament.

The most important thing in understanding the temple, or the tabernacle, is this: it is the holy place where God dwells. The word *shekinah* refers to the Holy Spirit, manifested in the cloud and in the fire. The word comes from the Hebrew root *shekhan*, 'to dwell'. That is where we get the word *mishkan*, 'God's dwelling place,' one of the words used for the temple.

John chapter one says, 'He dwelt among us.' The Greek word is *kataskenoo*, meaning 'to pitch a tent,' alluding to the Jewish idea of 'the dwelling'.

There are at least seven major tabernacles in the bible.

The first tabernacle is the one we call in Hebrew *ha ohel* 'the tent of meeting.' It was a dynamic tabernacle, designed to be portable by the Levites who would move it.

When it was pitched at night, the tribes of Israel would, in a configuration, camp around it according to their tribes (Numbers 2:1-31); the tribes, of course, being those of the patriarchs, the twelve sons of Jacob, the New Testament equivalent of the twelve apostles. The second tabernacle is the first temple, the temple of Solomon. The third is the second temple, the temple of Zerubbabel, later called Herod's temple when he expanded it. He actually used Ezekiel's vision of a temple as the blueprint to expand it along Greco-Roman lines to impress the Romans.

The fourth temple is the one that Ezekiel saw which, to the best of my understanding, is probably a millennial temple.

Jesus spoke of His physical body as a temple (John 2:19-21). This is the fifth temple.

The sixth tabernacle or temple is our body. *Do you not know that you are a temple of God, and that the Spirit of God dwells in you?* (1 Corinthians 3:16).

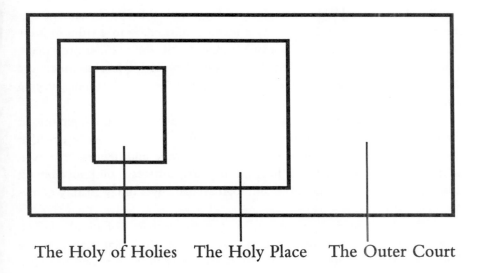

The Holy of Holies   The Holy Place   The Outer Court

The seventh, and final tabernacle is the church. In at least seven places in the New Testament—1 Corinthians 3:16,17; 6:19; 2 Corinthians 6:16; Ephesians 2:21; Revelation 13:6; 21:3—the church is called the tabernacle of God.

Each of these seven tabernacles follow this pattern: it is constructed as a box, within a box, within a box. There is the *sanctum sanctorum,* or the 'holy of holies.' In Hebrew it is called *ha kodesh kodeshim.* Then there is the outer chamber and a third chamber. Its sort of like a box, within a box, within a box.

Do you not know that your body is a temple of the Holy Spirit who is in you? (1 Corinthians 6:19). The *Outer Court* or the *Court of the Gentiles* corresponds to our physical bodies. It is what everyone sees and everyone has contact with. At the inside edge of the Outer Court during Jesus' time there were signs warning Gentiles not to go any further. Then there is the *Holy Place.* The Holy Place was entered by the Levites for sacrificial purposes. Then there is the *Holy of Holies,* where God's Spirit dwells.

It is important to understand this. If the Outer Court that everyone can see is our physical body, then the Holy Place is our soul: our emotions, our mind, our intellect. The Hebrew word is *nephesh.* Then inside our soul is another box. That is our spirit, our 'innermost man'. The New Testament usually alludes to it by the metaphor of 'the heart'; the Old Testament uses the term 'kidneys.' I saw a film by a medical missionary to a tribe in New Guinea which considered a person's throat to be their 'innermost man'. They would bury anyone who contracted laryngitis, because once the throat is gone, a person's life is over. The video shows them burying someone alive.

When these people got saved, they would ask Jesus into their throat. Even primordial peoples have a consciousness of an 'innermost man' that goes beyond the soul. Man is made in God's image and likeness and even people with no background in Judaism or Christianity can still know certain things about the one, true God, although secular psychology mainly denies it.

"Can Christians be demonised?" is a question that is often asked. The answer depends on what you mean by 'demonised.' Christians can be demonised in the Outer Court. Demons can afflict the bodies of Christians. They can even affect our emotions, our minds. Christians can be oppressed; they can be demonised in their minds. But a demon can never come into the innermost man. Only unsaved people can be demon possessed, whereby a demon occupies the innermost man instead of the Holy Spirit. The only way a bible believing Christian can have the innermost man entered by a demon is if he backslides beyond a terrible point, the way Saul did.

Unfortunately, some people involved in 'deliverance' do not make these distinctions and they wind up convincing Christians that they are demon possessed. There is a difference between oppression and possession. There is a limit to how far Satan can go in dealing with a believer. The temple followed a pattern of a box, within a box, within a box. There were things called 'walls of partition'. Sin brings separation. The most important wall of partition was the curtain between the Holy Place and the Holy of Holies, which was torn from top to bottom when Jesus was crucified (Matthew 27:51).

There was a wall of partition at the place where the priests entered, another at the place where the men entered, and another at the court of women.

Women were separated from men by a physical barrier. The clergy were separated from the men by a barrier, and the high priest was separated from the rest of the priests by a physical barrier. Around all of this there was a peripheral wall of partition, separating Jew from Gentile. Divisions between Jew and Gentile, divisions between men and women, divisions between the clergy and the lay people, and divisions between the ordinary clergy and the high priest are a result of the division between a holy God and unholy men.

The Jews thought that they were special because they were physically descended from Abraham. Jesus told them that was not true: God could raise up Abraham's children. out of the stones. Midrashically speaking, He was saying that He could make Gentile believers, Christians, into Abraham's descendants. On Palm Sunday the Jews cried out, "Hosanna, hosanna, to the Son of David". *And some of the Pharisees in the multitude said to Him, "Teacher, rebuke Your disciples". And He answered and said, "I tell you, if these become silent, the stones will cry out"* (Luke 19:39-40). He was saying, "If the Jews do not recognise me as the Messiah, the Christians will."

You also, as living stones, are being built up as a spiritual house for a holy priesthood (1 Peter 2:5).

We are the stones. The Hebrew word for 'fellowship' comes from the verb *chabar*, meaning 'to join together.' The reference is to bricks that have been cemented together. It is one thing to come to *church*, but it is very different to come *to fellowship*. If you come to church, you temporarily sit together. If you come to fellowship, you are cemented into a structure. A physical building with a brick missing here and a brick missing there is what a church is like if people are only coming to church and not to fellowship. There is a big difference.

For we are God's fellow workers, you are God's field, God's building (I Corinthians 3:9).

This is a Greek text, but Paul is drawing on the Hebrew idea of *binyon*, 'What God has built.' We are God's structure, God's building. The church is, once again, the temple.

Ephesians is probably the most important text in the New Testament for understanding the temple.

So then you are no longer strangers and aliens, but you are fellow citizens with the saints, and are of God's household, having been built upon the foundation of the apostles and prophets, Christ Jesus Himself being the corner stone, in whom the whole building, being fitted together is growing into a holy temple for the Lord; in whom you also are being built together into a dwelling of God in the Spirit (Ephesians 2:19-21).

Notice that the word *skenoo* in Greek, 'dwelling' is the same root as the Hebrew word *mishkan* or *shekinah,* meaning God in the Spirit. The church is to be the temple where God dwells. Never say there is no temple. There is a temple. Christians are the stones, Jesus is the corner stone and the apostles and prophets are the foundation stones. Look at the 'Hallel Rabbah' from Psalm 118:22 that they sang to Jesus on Palm Sunday. *The stone which the builders rejected is become the chief cornerstone.* Jesus is the cornerstone of this temple, the apostles and prophets are the foundation stones, and we are built on top of that.

There are five kinds of apostles in the bible. 'Apostle' in Hebrew is *sholakh,* the one who is 'sent' to establish a church. The Greek word is *apostolos,* meaning the same thing, one who is 'sent.'

First, Jesus is called *the Apostle,* the One who was sent, with the definite article. He is unique. All other apostolic authority must come from Jesus.

Second, there is the unique case of the twelve apostles. The twelve apostles correspond to the twelve patriarchs, or the twelve sons of Jacob in the Old Testament. As all the people of Israel were the descendants of the twelve tribes of Jacob, we, in some way, are the spiritual descendants of the twelve apostles.

In the Domitian Abbey in Jerusalem, there are three concentric circles cut up like a pie. In the innermost circle, there are the twelve patriarchs. In the middle circle, there are the twelve apostles, corresponding to them. So far, so good. But the third, outermost circle is the zodiac!

There is a lot of illuminati-type symbolism in the Roman Catholic churches in the Middle East.

The eye in the triangle and all this stuff makes you suspicious. I do not get into conspiracy theories the way some people do, but you cannot help but notice.

The apostles, then, are the foundation upon which the church is built. Jesus is *the* Apostle, and then there are the twelve apostles. Even Paul did not have all the qualifications of the original twelve. He affirmed that he was not the least of the apostles; his authority was co-equal with theirs (2 Corinthians 11:5). Yet he said he was the least because he had persecuted the church. In Revelation chapter 4, we see the twenty four elders. They are mentioned twice in Revelation. An educated guess as to who they are, would be that they are the twelve patriarchs and the twelve apostles. It is an eternally fixed number of which Paul is not a part. Third, when they looked for a replacement for Judas, they had to pick someone who had been around from the baptism of John (Acts 1:15-26). (John is a pivotal character in the inter-testamental relationship.) Paul had not been around from the baptism of John.

After the twelve apostles, there is the almost unique case of Paul. He had the same authority as they did, but did not match all of their requirements in every sense—having seen the Lord, and so on.

Fourth, in 1 Corinthians we see that there were other apostles. Paul was dealing with the problem of party spirit. He rebuked it, saying, Now I mean this, that each one of you is saying, "I am of Paul" and "I of Apollos", and "I of Cephas," and "I of Christ" (1 Corinthians 1:12).

There is Jesus, who is totally unique. There is Cephas (Peter), who was one of the twelve. There is Paul. And then there is the case of Apollos, a fourth kind. He was not like Paul, and he was certainly not like the twelve, but he had an apostolic ministry.

Fifth, there are people today who are apostles in this sense: they are church planting missionaries. They are not pastors. Once the church is established, they need to go somewhere else and establish another church. They are not very good pastors usually, but they are very good at planting churches.

In the context of Ephesians, the foundation stones mainly mean the twelve apostles, Paul, the apostles in the early church who wrote the bible, and the Old Testament prophets. The same process still holds true. If a church is planted, its foundation is going to be the apostle who planted it. In that sense apostolic authority can exist, but remember, the main New Testament thrust of apostolic authority is doctrine.

Does apostolic authority in the sense of the apostles exist today? Yes it does—in the New Testament. Apostolic authority is the teaching of the apostles. It is not heavy shepherding. It is not, "You do this and you do that." It is doctrine. Be careful of people in Restorationism who are appropriating to themselves the title of 'apostle,' thinking themselves to be somehow foundational, and assuming an authority that the Word of God or the Spirit of God gives to nobody. The only kind of apostles we have today are church planting missionaries. That is all.

Apostolic authority, as the apostles had it, is preserved in the doctrine of the New Testament. Apostolic authority was always concerned with doctrine, not with organisation or politics. Secondly, it was always plural, unlike the house churches, with their heavy shepherding and their leaders who claim to be "the apostle." The Holy Spirit said, *"Set apart for me Barnabas and Saul for the work to which I have called them"* (Acts 13:1). Jesus sent the apostles out in pairs (Mark 6:7). In the book of Acts, when they wanted to see what was happening in Samaria, they sent two apostles (Acts 8:14). Not only that but there was a mutual submission to the general council in Acts 15. Be careful of these head honchos who are appropriating to themselves the title of 'apostle'. This mentality exists in the house churches and, unfortunately, has come into much of pentecostalism, but it is not biblical.

But speaking the truth in love, we are to grow up in all aspects into Him, who is the Head, even Christ, from whom the whole body being fitted together by that which every joint supplies, according to the proper working, of each individual part, causes the growth of the body for the building up of itself in love (Ephesians 4:15–16).

Ephesians combines the language of architecture with the language of anatomy and structure. We are the body of Christ—bones, flesh, eyes, feet, etc.

How lovely on the mountains are the feet of him who brings good news who announces peace and brings good news of happiness, who announces salvation and says to Zion, your God reigns (Isaiah 52:7).

"How lovely on the mountains are the feet of him." That is what Paul is drawing on in Ephesians.

… having shod your feet with the preparation of the gospel of peace (Ephesians 6:15). We are the body of Christ. Who are the feet? They are the evangelists.

The lamp of your body is your eye; when your eye is clear, your whole body also is full of light (Luke 11). The eye sees. The eye is the teacher.

Good conduct is very important, but do you know what? The New Testament exhorts Christians to *right doctrine* twice as much as it exhorts them to *right conduct*.

Why? Because if you do not have right doctrine, you will not know what right conduct is.

"After these things I will return, and I will rebuild the tabernacle of David which has fallen, and I will rebuild its ruins, and I will restore it, in order that the rest of mankind may seek the Lord, and all the Gentiles who are called by My name," says the Lord, who makes these things known from of old (Acts 15:16–18).

This is a prophecy taken from Amos 9:11, out of the Septuagint, the Greek Old Testament.

"After these things I will return and I will rebuild the tabernacle of David which has fallen, and I will rebuild its ruins, and I will restore it."

Before the temple was built by Solomon, David's tabernacle was the tent that was in Shiloh. David's tabernacle was *dynamic*. It was meant to be transported, even though it was usually found in Shiloh. Amos predicted that the tabernacle of David would be restored.

Somehow we would go from a fixed building back to something dynamic. Both the text and the context of Acts 15 shows that the dynamic structure which fulfils the prophecy is the church. The church has re-established the mobile tabernacle of David.

And recognising the grace that had been given to me, James and Cephas and John, who were reputed to be pillars, gave to me and Barnabas the right hand of fellowship, that we might go to the Gentiles, and they to the circumcised (Galatians 2:9).

The original twelve apostles recognised the apostolic ministry of Paul and Barnabas, but the twelve apostles were said to be 'pillars'. There were two pillars in the temple, "Boaz" and "Jakin" (1 Kings 7:21). *Boaz* means 'in His strength,' and *Jakin* means 'he will establish' or 'Yahweh will establish.' Pillars hold the roof up. If the pillars go, the roof collapses. If apostolic authority goes, the building will collapse.

Unfortunately, apostolic authority is going. Why? Because, the church is departing from the teaching of the apostles into Restorationist theology, with its false concept of apostolic authority.

Notice that physical components of the temple are identified with different kinds of Christians.

He who overcomes, I will make him a pillar in the temple of my God (Revelation 3).

There is no temple in the eternal city. There is a tabernacle because Jesus is there; the whole place is a tabernacle, but not a building, not a temple as such.

This has something to do with the church because there is no temple in heaven: a tabernacle, yes, but not a temple (Revelation 21:22). The people who overcome will be the pillars.

To be a real apostle, to be a real church planter, you have to be somebody who is, above all things, an overcomer. Look at the lives of the apostles. They were overcomers. They were people who faced terrible opposition, persecution, heresy, and betrayal, but they overcame.

In so many places, over and over, the New Testament defines the church, or identifies the church, as the tabernacle. God has always had a tabernacle, ever since the first one, but now it is us. Jesus spoke of His body as the temple. *"Destroy this temple and I will raise it again in three days"* (John 2:19). But the church is the body of Christ. What happens to Him, happens to us.

The Hebrew language is usually dependent on three letters, sometimes two but usually three, called the *shoresh,* which means 'root.' When any two words have the same root, they are connected etymologically, and they are often connected theologically. The root of Hosea, *Hoshea,* is *shin.* Isaiah is *Yeshiyahu.* Joshua is *Yehoshua.* Jesus is *Yeshua.* Whenever the *sh* sound occurs in Hebrew, it means something to do with salvation.

He will revive us after two days; He will raise us up on the third day that we may live before Him (Hosea 6:2).

His resurrection is replayed, or recapitulated, in the experience of the church in the last days. Jesus said, *"Destroy this temple and I will raise it again in three days"* (John *2:19).* That happened to His temple—His body, and somehow it also happens to us.

This is very important when you read Matthew 24. They were marvelling at the stones of the Herodian temple, and He said, "not one stone will be thrown down upon another." Jesus was referring back to the prophecies of the prophet Daniel, chapter 9. The Messiah would have to come and die before the second temple would be destroyed. Somehow that destruction of the temple is a type of what happens to the church at the end. The stones are thrown down, but then resurrected in glory to an eternal temple, the way His body was. We are made in God's image and likeness. We are a tri-unity. We are the outer court, the holy place and the holy of holies, because God is triune. Jesus is God's prototype. We are made in His image. He was a temple, so we are a temple.

When you understand temple narrative and the temple typology, you understand the reasons why God said that marriage is to be held sacrosanct and to let the marriage bed remain undefiled.

If you are a Christian and you have a wife, her body is a temple of the Holy Spirit. You do not enter God's temple irreverently. It does not mean that it is not erotic. It does not mean that it is not fun. It does mean that it is not to be with sin. It is God's temple.

Somehow, sexuality in marriage is like the high priest going into the temple, or it is Jesus going inside His bride, the church, causing the church to be fruitful. We are made in His image and likeness. Sex replays spiritual things. "Keep the marriage bed undefiled."

"Don't you know that you are a temple of the Holy Spirit?" Hassidic Jews understand this idea. They say that the *Shekinah* dwells over the marriage bed when a couple is making love. They understand that there is this spiritual aspect to it and that God's Spirit hovers over it.

Now Hiram [who was a Gentile] *king of Tyre sent his servants to Solomon, when he heard that they had anointed him king in place of his father, for Hiram had always been a friend of David* (1 Kings 5:1).

Right here there is a picture of camaraderie between Jew and Gentile. Remember that David is usually a type of Jesus. Jesus is called *Yeshua ben David* (Jesus the Son of David).

Then Solomon sent word to Hiram, saying, "You know that David my father was unable to build a house for the Name of the Lord his God because, of the wars which surrounded him, until the Lord put them under the soles of his feet. But now the Lord my God has given me rest on every side; there is neither adversary nor misfortune. And behold, I intend to build a house for the name of the Lord my God, as the Lord spoke to David my father, saying, 'Your son, whom I will set on your throne in your place, he will build the house for my Name.' Now therefore, command that they cut for me cedars from Lebanon, and my servants will be with your servants; and I will give you wages for your servants according to all that you say for you know that there is no one among us who knows how to cut timber like the Sidonians." (1 Kings 5:2-6).

Nobody knows how to cut down trees like the Gentiles.

And it came about when Hiram heard the words of Solomon, that he rejoiced greatly and said, 'Blessed be the Lord today, who has given to David a wise son over this great people.' So Hiram sent word to Solomon, saying, *'I have heard the message which you have sent me; I will do what you desire concerning the cedar and cypress timber. My servants will bring them down from Lebanon to the sea, and I will make them into rafts to go by sea to the place where you direct me, and I will have them broken up there, and you shalt carry them away. Then you shall accomplish my desire by giving food to my household'* (1 Kings 5:7). Remember that the Phoenicians were very good sailors.

So Hiram gave Solomon as much as he desired of the cedar and cypress timber (1 Kings 5:10).

David had left the gold and silver that Solomon needed to build the temple. He received from his father that which he needed, but then he used the Gentiles to bring in more of what he needed to build this temple.

Solomon then gave Hiram 20,000 kors of wheat as food for his household, and twenty kors of beaten oil; thus Solomon would give Hiram year by year. The Lord gave wisdom to Solomon, just as He promised him, and there was peace between Hiram and Solomon, and the two of them made a covenant (1 Kings 5:11-12).

Solomon is the son of David who caused peace between Jew and Gentile. But lasting peace between Jew and Gentile was something that would only come from Jesus, the Son of David.

And now send me a skilled man to work in gold, silver, brass and iron, and in purple, crimson and violet fabrics, and who knows how to make engravings, to work with the skilled men whom I have in Judah and Jerusalem, whom David my father provided (2 Chronicles 2:7).

The colours and the precious minerals have special significance. The further into the temple you went, and the closer you drew to the Holy of Holies, the greater the cost of the minerals with which it was constructed. The progression was from brass to silver to gold.

Brass has to do with fire. The brazen altar was made of brass and was a type of the cross. The only way we can get to God is through the cross, which makes atonement for sin.

It is interesting that the brazen altar was made from the mirrors of women (Exodus 38:8). They did not have glass in those days. Mirrors were made from a kind of copper which was burnished—polished and polished and polished, until you could see your face reflected in it. Somehow the idea was that they gave their own vanity over to the Lord's service, for His purposes, realising that the vanity of man was useless. They used the things of the flesh, that would exalt themselves, to make a cross.

Silver always has to do with the price of redemption. Jesus was betrayed for thirty pieces of silver (Matthew 26:15). The Levites had to redeem their first born with silver (Numbers 18:15-16).

Then, in the innermost, is gold. *An excellent wife is the crown of her husband* (Proverbs 12:4).

Gold is the godliness. The diamonds are something forged with fire. When we sing the hymn, "Crown Him with many crowns," alluding to Revelation, that is the church crowning Jesus.

The church is the crown of the husband, it is His glory. The church is supposed to be the glory of Jesus, like the crown is to a king's head—the gold inset with precious stones that have been forged by fire.

That is one of the reasons why we go through trials. It is the fire that perfects the stones.

There is a typology of the colours and minerals. The minerals correspond to the walls and the different kinds of stones that are in Revelation—emeralds, sardonyx, rubies etc. The colours also correspond eg. crimson.

Though your sins be as scarlet, they shall be as white as snow; though they are red like crimson, they will be like wool (Isaiah 1:18).

Purple is the priestly colour. Blue is the royal colour. They all have meanings. Solomon needed people who knew how to work these things.

Send me also cedar, cypress and algum timber from Lebanon, for I know that your servants know how to cut timber of Lebanon; and indeed, my servants will work with your servants, to prepare timber in abundance for me, for the house which I am about to build will be great and wonderful.

Now behold, I will give your servants, the woodsmen who cut the timber, 20,000 kors of crushed wheat, and 20,000 kors of barley, and 20,000 baths of wine, and 20,000 baths of oil (2 Chronicles 2:8-10).

Let's begin with the trees. Jesus healed the blind man, who said that he saw men "like trees, walking about" (Mark 8:24). *The trees of the field* [the mission field] *will clap their hands* (Isaiah 55:12). We shall be called *"trees of righteousness"* (Isaiah 61:3). *A good tree cannot produce bad fruit, nor can a bad tree produce good fruit* (Matthew 7:18). Trees represent different things in the bible in different places. Here they represent God's people.

Our grain is the word of God, it is our spiritual food. "Cast much bread upon the water." "The bread that I give you."

Different liquids represent the Holy Spirit in different aspects. Jesus said that He would give the woman at the well "living water" (John 4:10). Isaiah 44:3 shows us that "living water" is God's Spirit. *But this He spoke of the Spirit* (John 7:39). Living water is the Holy Spirit in one aspect. *"You shall not thirst again"*. It shall flow out from us. Wine is the joy of the Spirit. Oil is the anointing of the Holy Spirit. The Holy Spirit is typified, or represented, by different liquids in different contexts in scripture.

So look at what we have here. There is peace between Jew and Gentile and they are building this immense structure together; they are going to build a house for the Lord. Stones, pillars, trees. Different structural components of the temple represent different kinds of Christians.

The Jews had the blueprint. David gave the blueprint to his son, as the Father gave the blueprint to His Son (both are the Son of David).

The Jews had the grain. The Jews had the oil. The Jews had the precious stones. The Jews had the gold. Jews had the silver. The Jews had the fabric.

The Gentiles had the numbers. The Gentiles had the 'know how.' The Gentiles had the manpower. The temple never could have been built by the Jews alone. It never could have been built by the Gentiles alone. There had to be a reconciliation between Jew and Gentile to build this temple. The Jews could not do it without the Gentiles, and the Gentiles could not do it without the Jews. They were mutually dependent upon each other.

Nobody knows how to cut down trees like the Gentiles. Who are the biggest soul winners in history? Since the early church almost all of them have been Gentiles. The great evangelists: Spurgeon, Billy Graham, D.L. Moody, the Wesleys, George Whitefield—nobody knows how to cut down a tree like a *goy* (Gentile).

Not only that, but they floated the trees on the sea. The earth usually corresponds to Israel, but the sea corresponds to the nations. The Gentiles brought the trees to Jerusalem.

Cedars of Lebanon and cypress trees are types of Gentile Christians. Most of the structure of the temple was made up of these trees. The biggest part of the temple was Gentile, but its foundation was built by Jews. The foundation is under the ground.

My grandparents were from the north of England. I was born in New

York where they have skyscrapers: more than one thousand of them in Manhatten alone. The tallest London building would not be considered impressive in Manhatten. When they build a skyscraper, they display a picture of what it is going to look like on the boards they put around the construction site. Then they dig through the rock, deeper and deeper. This goes on for months. You start to think that the building will never be completed.

Then, all of a sudden, the girders are up, practically overnight, and next thing you know, there is the building. How did it get there so fast?

The most important thing was getting the foundation right. You cannot construct a one hundred story building without a deep, solid foundation.

God dealt with the Jews for two thousand years to give birth to the church. It took a very long time but, once that foundation was there, what happened on the day of pentecost? Bang! There it was. There was the building. You do not see the foundation stones. They are under the ground. But, when you see a hundred story building, you know that there must be a very strong, deep foundation. Even though you do not see it, you know it is there, otherwise the building could not exist.

The church is no different. It has a very strong and a very deep foundation, built by the Jews. It is similar to the argument in Romans chapter 11. You do not see the roots, but they are there. If the roots were not there, the tree would die. If God is finished with the Jews, He must also be finished with the church. It does not matter what the Restorationists tell you.

Jews and Gentiles working together. The Gentiles had the 'know how,' the Gentiles had the manpower and the ability to bring the trees by sea to Jerusalem—a type of the heavenly Jerusalem. What did the Jews give the Gentiles? The blueprint, the grain, and the oil (the Holy Spirit was poured out on the Jews on the day of Pentecost). Remember Jeremiah 31. *"I will make a new covenant with the house of Israel and the house of Judah"*—not with the baptists, not with the pentecostals. The new covenant is made with the Jews. The Jews gave the Word of God to the Gentiles. The Jews gave the blueprint. The Jews provided the foundation, but then the Gentiles built the building. That was God's plan from the beginning. Paul called it the *"mystery"* of the gospel—peace and reconciliation between Jew and Gentile 'in order to build a temple to our God'. That was always His plan, right from the beginning.

The church is also called the 'tabernacle of David,' from Amos. It is to be dynamic. The "coming out of Egypt" spoke of the church coming out of the world on its way to heaven, with the Holy Spirit leading them. The Egyptians gave them the materials that were later used in constructing the tabernacle. God takes the things of the world and uses them for His glory.

Will the temple be rebuilt? Over and over the bible teaches that the church is the temple. In the book of Acts they were meeting in Solomon portico. The temple was under the sentence of death because of Daniel 9. But while this temple was under the sentence of death, God was already rebuilding another one right next to it—the church. When the new one was ready, the old one came down. It had to come down. Why? *The Holy Spirit is signifying this, that the way into the holy place has not yet been disclosed, while the outer tabernacle is still standing* (Hebrews 9:8).

The destruction of the physical temple, as predicted by Daniel, happened in 70AD; you can read the accounts in Josephus. It was reiterated by Jesus in the Olivet discourse (Matthew 24, Luke 21). The destruction of the physical temple was simply a natural reflection of the destruction of Jesus' body. After Jesus had been nailed to the cross for our sins, the natural temple had to be destroyed.

The *mishnah* tells us that on *Yom Kippur*, the Day of Atonement, a scarlet thread was hung before the Holy of Holies. If the people's sins were forgiven, the scarlet thread would turn white. If the people's sins were not forgiven; the thread would remain crimson. The Talmud tells us that for forty years before the temple was destroyed (in other words, from the time that Jesus was crucified), the scarlet thread did not turn white, the people's sins were not forgiven under the law.

The temple had to be destroyed, because as long as it stood it represented separation—the separation of sinful man from holy God, the separation of the high priest from the clergy, the separation of the clergy from the people, the separation of men from women, the separation of Jew from Gentile.

For we are His workmanship, created in Christ Jesus for good works, which God prepared beforehand, that we should walk in them (Ephesians 2:10).

You were not only saved to go to heaven, you were saved to do something in this world. You are like one of Solomon's workers if you are

Jewish, or like one of Hiram's workers if you are Gentile. God has some work for you to do in building this temple.

The book of Nehemiah carries the same idea—different groups of people worked together rebuilding the walls of Jerusalem. Remember that you were saved to build something in this temple. If you do not put that brick in, the brick is not going to be there. God will have to get somebody else to do what He had for you to do. Before you were born again, before the world was created, there was something that God had in mind for you to do in building this temple. There is no born again Christian in the world that God does not have something for them to do. You were saved to serve. This is why scripture distinguishes between our salvation and our calling; both are ordained from eternity (2 Timothy 1:9).

Therefore remember, that formerly [that is, under the old covenant] *you, the Gentiles in the flesh, who are called "uncircumcision" by the so-called "circumcision," which is performed in the flesh by human hands—remember that you were at that time separate from Christ, excluded from the commonwealth of Israel and strangers to the covenants of promise, having no hope and without God in the world. But now in Christ Jesus...* ['Christ Jesus' is different to 'Jesus Christ.' 'Christ Jesus' always has to do with Him after He has been glorified] *you who formerly were far off have been brought near by the blood of Christ. For He Himself is our peace, who made both groups into one, and broke down the barrier of the dividing wall, by abolishing in His flesh the enmity, which is the Law of commandments contained in ordinances, that in Himself He might make the two into one new man, thus establishing peace, and might reconcile them both in one body to God through the cross, by it having put to death the enmity* (Ephesians 2:11-16).

There is no way into the Holy Place when the outer one is standing. Because Jesus' body was destroyed, the temple had to be destroyed. The temple represents the division between Jew and Gentile. When Jesus died, He got rid of that division, so the temple, which was designed to teach people about it, went as well.

And He came and preached peace to you who were far away [that is, the Gentiles], *and peace to those who were near* [that is, the Jews]; *for through Him we both have our access in one Spirit to the Father.*

So then you are no longer strangers and aliens, but you are fellow-citizens with the saints, and are of God's household, having been built on the foundations of the apostles and prophets, Christ Jesus Himself being the cornerstone, in whom the whole building, being fitted together is growing into a holy temple in the Lord; in whom you also are being built together into a dwelling [drawing on the same Hebrew idea, *mishkan* from the Hebrew, *kataskenoo* from the Greek] *of God in the Spirit* (Ephesians 2:17).

Jesus said, "Destroy the temple and I will raise it up," speaking of His body. The old temple was destroyed; the new one, the church meeting in Solomon's Portico, was raised up in its place. Jesus' physical body was crucified, but His glorified body was created in its place. Somehow the church, at the end, will be crucified, but then resurrected to victory. It is the same pattern.

Because of sin, these barriers exist. When Jesus died, the natural temple had to be destroyed. Why? Because when He died, Gentile would no longer be separated from Jew, and therefore the natural wall of partition had to be knocked down. He is our reconciliation. The wall of partition is broken down. He is our peace. We shall be one. In Jerusalem, even in the midst of the Intifada and the hatred, you can see meetings with Jew and Arab together, singing in Hebrew, in Arabic, and in English, "He is our peace".

The orthodox Jews pray, "Thank God I was not born a dog or a Gentile or a woman." There are differences between men and women, different functions, but by the standards of the ancient world, the Jews gave women a much higher place than Gentiles did.

If you want to see what women were like outside of Judaism, or in the pre-Christian Middle East, look at the moslem culture. Nobody says anything about the way little girls are abused by their brothers. In a place like rural Egypt, in the villages, a man will have a camel whip up on his wall. Is that for his camel? No. It is for his wife. He can divorce her and get the kids under Islamic law and she has no claim to anything. All he has to do is say three times, "I divorce you," and she is legally finished.

These guys make their wives strip and they beat them. That is how women were treated in much of the ancient world. The Jews gave women rights under *Halachah* that were not found outside of the Jewish context, usually, in the ancient world. Then Christianity was almost like feminism—with Paul saying that women are co-equal in Christ, and co-heirs in Christ, and Peter saying, "Submit to one other in love." This does not mean that the husband is not the head, but it does mean that a wife is a co-heir. These ideas were radical. The Jewish idea gave women a much higher status than most of the Gentile ideas of what women were supposed to be like. But then the church brought something totally, radically different again.

The Greek idea was that every man should have three women. He should have a concubine - who would basically be a sex object, he would have a mistress—for intellectual compatibility, and he would have a wife—who would be the mother of his children. Now in the Christian design, the same woman would fulfil all three functions. It went totally against the Greek idea and it went against the Jewish idea, which was already superior to the Gentile one. The wall of partition is broken down.

That does not mean that I believe in women pastors. I do not. We are still living in a fallen world, and men and women are both under the curse of the fall. Women are very vulnerable to spiritual seduction, more so than men. They are very sensitive and they can hear the voice of the Holy Spirit more easily than men can.

When a husband and wife pray together, it will usually be the wife that God speaks through. When a husband and wife get saved, it is usually the wife who gets saved first. But because women are more sensitive and it is easier for them to hear the voice of the Holy Spirit, it is also easier for them to hear the voice of another spirit. The serpent beguiled the woman. Women are much more vulnerable by nature to spiritual seduction. That is the idea of headship.

God's idea of headship is protection, not domination or dominion. The husband is head of the wife as Christ is head of the church. A husband is expected by God to give himself for his wife, the way that Christ laid His life down for the church. On the other hand, she has to recognise his responsibility and authority. It is a protective model. It is not master/slave, or whatever you want to call it. That is the world's mentality.

So the wall of partition between Jew and Gentile had to go. And then the one between men and women had to go.

But then the wall that separates the clergy from the lay people had to go. We are all priests. "He will purify the priests of Levi", it says in Isaiah. We are all priests, a kingdom of priests.

Before Satan paganised the church, he Judaised it. Roman Catholicism is based on two corruptions of the church: Judaisation and paganisation.

The paganisation came later, after Constantine mainly. The Judaisation came first. Instead of a priesthood of all believers, they reintroduced a separate priesthood, going back under the law in a way that Paul warned against in Galatians. The whole Church of England is split over the question of women priests. The question is not, "Should we have women priests?" The question is, "Why should we have priests at all?" The bible says that all believers are priests. The whole issue is superfluous.

Before Satan paganised the church, he Judaised it. Instead of having a tabernacle like David's, where God's Spirit moves, the Catholics say that He is in the church building in a little box on the 'altar' called the 'tabernacle' where they put the 'eucharist'. They say, "That is where He dwells".

It is a return to the Law.

Roman Catholicism is a Judaisation and a paganisation of Christianity. *You foolish Galatians, who has bewitched you?* (Galatians 3:1). This false teaching has to go because it separates the clergy from the people.

Then the veil had to go. It separated holy God from sinful man. Jesus became our righteousness. We are counted righteous through repentance and faith in Him. So the separation between man and God goes.

Jesus died to break down the wall of partition between Jew and Gentile, between men and women, between clergy and lay people and, ultimately, between holy God and sinful man.

When Jesus died, the temple veil was torn from the top to the bottom. Notice that it began internally. God always begins on the inside and works outward. The world does the opposite: it goes from the outside and tries to work inward. Even when God gave the blueprint for building the tent of meeting, He began on the inside and worked outward.

Jesus has raised up a new temple where Jew will no longer be separated from Gentile, men no longer separated from women, clergy no longer separated from lay people, and sinful man no longer separated from a holy God.

Will another temple be built, based on Second Thessalonians? The likelihood is that it will, but remember that when the physical temple was destroyed in 70AD it was only a reflection of the deeper spiritual truth that you read about in Hebrews chapter 9.

Access to the innermost Holy of Holies was not possible until the outer one, of which it was a type, was still standing. It says directly in Hebrews that this temple is a copy of things in the heavens. The destruction of this physical temple was only a reflection of something spiritual.

When the veil before the Holy of Holies was torn, a physical event happened in the physical temple, which was only a reflection of a deeper spiritual truth: that sinful man was no longer separated from holy God, because Jesus paid the price,

If the physical temple, is rebuilt, and an abomination of desolation is set up, it will only reflect a deeper spiritual truth.

When you see the Archbishop of Canterbury involved in "interfaith worship" in a Christian church, the abomination of desolation has already begun. When you see homosexual clergy, that is the abomination of desolation. When you see a bishop denying the resurrection of Jesus Christ, and two thirds of the other bishops defend him, that is the abomination of desolation.

I have no doubt in my mind that the Antichrist will be worshipped in christendom. But if the physical temple is rebuilt, with an image set up in it, it will only be a reflection of what is really going on.

When you see the archaeologists from Hebrew University digging underneath the mosque of Omar, looking to rebuild the temple, it is simply a reflection of what is happening in Canterbury Cathedral, or in St James, Picadilly, or any of the other New Age churches. Will the temple be rebuilt?

The temple has already been rebuilt: it is us. It is not the building of a physical temple that concerns me, but the abomination of desolation already being set up in the temple.

CHRISTIAN ZIONISM

*N*OW *when they had come together, they were asking Him, saying, "Lord is it at this time that you are restoring the kingdom to Israel?" He said to them, "It is not for you to know the times or epochs which the Father has fixed by His own authority but you shall receive power when the Holy Spirit is come upon you; and you shall be My witnesses, both in Jerusalem, and in all Judea and Samaria, and even to the remotest parts of the earth"* (Acts 1-8).

Those were the final word of Jesus. I have two first names. When I was a baby they called me *James*. It was anglicised from my father's grandfather's name, *Ya'akov*, and *Jacob*. It is good that I have two first names because my family is a combination of two backgrounds—Irish Catholics and Jews.

My wife is a Romanian Jew. She was a *refusenik* under the communists. She immigrated to Israel as a kid. Her parents are holocaust survivors; the rest of the family were killed by the Nazis. My wife suffered under the communists as a child. Her parents knew nothing but anti-semitism the whole of their lives.

Our children were born in Israel, in Galilee. I understand both sides. I understand things from the Jewish perspective, and I understand the way Gentile Christians who love Israel feel. I can see things both ways because of my background. It helps to understand why the disciples asked Jesus that last question and why He answered it as He did. In Judaism there are two pictures of the Messiah, as the rabbis later defined it: *Ha Mashiach ben David* (the Messiah the Son of David) and *Ha Mashiach ben Yosef* (the Messiah the Son of Joseph).

The son of Joseph is the suffering servant Messiah of Isaiah 52 & 53. The son of David is the conquering king Messiah, who will set up the Kingdom.

The rabbis who wrote the Talmud understood that the Messiah was to come in the character of both David and Joseph.

Joseph was betrayed by his Jewish brothers into the hands of Gentiles. God took that betrayal, turned it around, and made it a way for all Israel and all the world to be saved. Jesus, the Son of David, was betrayed by His Jewish brothers into the hands of Gentiles. God took that betrayal and turned it around and made it a way for all Israel and all the world to be saved.

Joseph was the beloved son of his father. Jesus, the son of Joseph was the beloved son of His Father.

Joseph knew the wickedness of his brothers. Jesus, the son of Joseph knew the wickedness of His brothers.

Joseph was condemned with two criminals, and as he prophesied, one lived, and one died.

Jesus, the son of Joseph, was condemned with two criminals, and as He prophesied, one lived and one died.

They brought Joseph's tunic to prove he was not in the pit. They brought Jesus' shroud to prove He was not in the tomb.

Joseph went from a place of condemnation to a place of exaltation in a single day. Jesus, the son of Joseph, went from a place of condemnation, to a place of exaltation in a single day.

When Joseph was exalted every knee had to bow to him, and when

Jesus is exalted, every knee shall bow to Him.

Joseph was betrayed by his brother Judah (Judas) for twenty pieces of silver. After inflation, the Lord Jesus, the son of Joseph, was betrayed by His brother Judas for thirty pieces of silver.

And I will pour out upon the house of David and on the inhabitants of Jerusalem, the Spirit of grace and of supplication, so that they will look upon Me whom they have pierced; and they will mourn for Him, as one mourns for an only son, and they will weep bitterly over Him, like the bitter weeping over a first-born (Zechariah 12:10).

Joseph's brothers did not recognise him at his first coming. They recognised him at the second and wept bitterly.

Jesus' brothers, the Jews, did not recognise Him at the first coming. They are going to recognise Him at the second, and weep bitterly. The one they rejected and betrayed is the one who is going to save us in the great tribulation—the Son of Joseph.

Most Jews reject Jesus for two reasons. The first reason – and the one that intimidates Gentiles the most is the easiest to deal with, the unfortunate history of Christian anti-semitism. It sounds intimidating, yet it is the easiest objection to deal with. An orthodox Jew murdered Yitzak Rabin in the name of the Torah. Do you reject Moses and the Torah because of what somebody did in his name? Well, don't expect me to blame Jesus for what somebody did in His name! The murderer of Rabin perverted the teachings of Moses and the Torah. And nazi anti-semites perverted the teachings of Jesus to do the same thing to the Jews. More than that, Jews murdered their own prophets in the name of the Torah.

The second objection is more difficult. If He is the Messiah, how come He did not set up the messianic kingdom and bring in worldwide peace? The Messiah is supposed to be 'the Prince of Peace'.

The answer is found in Daniel chapter nine: The Messiah had to come and die before the second temple was destroyed. Wars and desolation are determined to the end. The purpose of His second coming is to set up His kingdom and bring in worldwide peace. The purpose of His first coming was to bring peace to the hearts of those who repent and accept Him as their Messiah.

From a Jewish perspective, the Messiah must fulfil all the Old Testament Messianic prophecies—both the Son of David ones and the Son of Joseph ones.

The Son of David prophecies have only been fulfilled in a spiritual sense. Jesus did not bring in worldwide peace and fulfil those prophecies historically.

In other words, if He is not going to come back and set up the millennial Kingdom, He is not the Messiah of the Jews. And if He is not the Messiah of the Jews, neither is He the Christ of the church.

Forget all this amillennial, post-millennial hogwash. It is an invention of Roman Catholicism, with no biblical basis. All of the pre-Nicean fathers held to pre-millennial eschatology, and also said that the apostles held pre-millennial views. It was only after Constantine 'Christianised' the Roman Empire and made it the religion of the state, that they began saying Israel was spiritualised in the church. And the Kingdom Now, Dominionist rubbish you see today is part of the same post-millennialist error that has been around since Constantine's day.

If there is no millennium, Jesus is not the Messiah of the Jews. And if He is not the Messiah of the Jews, neither is He the Christ of the church. A Jewish understanding of eschatology can allow for nothing but pre-millennialism. So what the apostles were saying here is, 'When are you going to set up the kingdom?' The last thing Jesus said is, 'That's God's worry. You let God worry about restoring the kingdom.'

The bible never says the kingdom will be restored to *the church*. It says the Kingdom will be restored to Israel. Replacement theology (which says that the church has replaced Israel in God's plan) is false!

The Jews going back to Israel is the fulfilment of what Jesus said: *Jerusalem will be trampled underfoot by the Gentiles until the time of the Gentiles be fulfilled* (Luke 21:24). It is one of many signs that Jesus gave to let us know that the end is near. If the devil cannot blind people to pre-millennialism and the prophetic purposes of God for Israel and the Jews, he is going to blind them the other way. Instead of worrying about what Jesus said to worry about, they worry about things He said not to worry about!

Suppose your husband was in the navy and he was going away and you were not going to see him for a year. He kisses you goodbye and walks out the door. The last thing he tells you should be the thing you remember the most.

Jesus is the Bridegroom. He is the Husband. The last thing He said is the thing the church is forgetting the most. On the one hand we have people forgetting that the kingdom must be restored to Israel—that is the post-millennial, kingdom Now, Replacement theology types—but on the other hand we have Christian Zionism. when are you restoring the kingdom. That is God's worry! What is your worry? Evangelism! *Be My witnesses both in Jerusalem, and in all Judea and Samaria, and even to the remotest parts of the earth* (Acts 1:8).

You let God worry about bringing the Jews back to Israel and restoring the kingdom, you worry about giving them the gospel.

Today, we have sincere, honest people, many of whom have a genuine love for Israel, that are doing the opposite.

One of the most difficult questions I get asked around the world is this: 'How come Dr Arnold Fruchtenbaum, the leading Jewish Christian scholar in the world is so much against the International Christian Embassy? How come Jews for Jesus are so much against the International Christian Embassy? How come so many Israeli pastors are against the International Christian Embassy? How come so many of the leading Jewish Christians in the world have written articles against it?' [Just read issue 12 of *Mishkan,* the Messianic theological journal]. Because they are doing the opposite of what Jesus said. Organisations funded by ICEJ have signed agreements to not give the gospel to the Jews, in order to obtain government cooperation in bringing Jews back to Israel. Another such organisation is *'Bridges for Peace'*, but there can be no peace biblically between Jew and Gentile except via the salvation of the Prince of Peace who breaks down the partition (Ephesians 2:14).

The International Christian Embassy people took Morris Cerullo and 'Toronto' to Israel, but some of them are very sincere. I do not question the love or sincerity of these people. But they are caught up in a big deception. They say that, by denying the gospel to the Jews that they rescue, they are able to get the cooperation of the rabbis, the Jewish Agency, and the Israeli government.

There are many people involved in bringing Jews back to Israel. The biggest ones are *Jonathan and David* and *Prayer for Israel.* Two others are Sister Alice and Beryl Hunter. The people who bring the most Jews out do not look for the cooperation of the rabbis—or the Israeli government, because they are not willing to compromise giving the gospel to the Jews.

I believe in getting the Jews out of Russia, but I also believe in getting them out of hell. Yitzak Rabin knew many Christian Zionists. They shook his hand, applauded him, and ingratiated themselves. If Yitzak Rabin could come back for five or ten seconds, do you know what he would say? "You people said you loved me, my nation and my people. But you let me enter eternity and stand before the judgement seat of my Messiah without having His blood to atone for my sins! If you loved me, why did you let me die without my Messiah?"

What did Paul say about Jewish evangelism in Acts? *I am innocent of the blood of all men. For I did not shrink from declaring to you the whole purpose of God* (Acts 20:26-27).

When I say to the wicked, "You shall surely die"; and you do not warn him or speak out to warn the wicked from his wicked way that he may live, that wicked man shall die in his iniquity, but his blood I will require at your hand (Ezekiel 3:18).

The founder of one such organisation that signed an agreement not to tell Jews the gospel called 'Ebenezer Fund' literally brought this curse on himself and his arm was amputated.

In context, God is speaking to Ezekiel about Israel. If you do not warn them, I will require their blood from your hands! Withholding the gospel is not a form of love. Paul had a biblical definition of love for the Jews. *My heart's desire... is for their salvation* (Romans 10:1)

Could you imagine St Paul signing an agreement to not evangelise Jews and telling Christians to not preach the gospel to them? Just get them back to Israel and God will save them! I cannot. The ICEJ say they can justify trying to bless Israel and the Jews without giving them the gospel.

"Comfort, O comfort My people," says your God. "Speak kindly to Jerusalem. Call out to her, that her warfare has ended, that her iniquity has been removed, that she has received of the Lord's hand double for all her sins" (Isaiah 40:1-2).

Isaiah goes on and explains how to comfort His people. *Get yourself up on a high mountain, O Zion, bearer of good news...* (Isaiah 40:9). The Hebrew word for "good news" is *bisorah*—good news, the gospel.

Lift up your voice mightily O Jerusalem, bearer of good news, lift it up, do not fear. Say to the cities of Judah, "Here is your God" (Isaiah 40:9).

He says it twice. How do you comfort His people? Tell them the gospel. You say, "Here is the gospel; here is the *bisorah*, here is your God the Messiah." That is the biblical method for comforting God's people. Do you think that Israel's iniquity can be removed by anything other than the blood of the Messiah? There is no other name under heaven by which men can be saved. *The gospel is the power of God for salvation to everyone who believes, to the Jew first and also to the Greek* (Romans 1:16).

How lovely on the mountains are the feet of him who brings good news [bisorah], *who announces peace and brings good news* [bisorah] *of happiness, who announces salvation* (Isaiah 52:7).

Jesus—*Yeshua*—is salvation. How do you comfort God's people? Tell them about Jesus! Not every Christian has the gift of preaching or the gift of teaching. But would you refuse to read the bible because you do not have the gift of teaching?

Not every Christian is a pastor. Would you refuse to act as the spiritual head and shepherd of your family because you are not called as a pastor? It is just as wrong to refuse to witness because you do not have the gift of evangelism.

It is true that we cannot all stand on a podium and preach to a large group and see numbers saved, but there is nobody who cannot witness one on one. Let the redeemed of the Lord say so!

Romans 9:9-11 is the heart of God's purpose for Israel and the Jews, and the relationship between Israel and the church. Read Romans 9:9-11. There is no emphasis on national restoration in it. None! National restoration is subordinate to Israel's salvation. The Jews are being regathered to Israel, not for a blessing, but for the "time of Jacob's trouble", the great tribulation. They are being regathered for a holocaust. They are going to be deceived by the Antichrist.

Jesus said, *"I have come in My Father's name, and you do not receive Me, another shall come in his own name, you will receive him"* (John 5:43).

The only way the Jews will have the peace they long for is by turning to the Prince of Peace. Jews who accept Jesus will have that peace. There is no peace outside of Jesus.

The regathering of Israel is a sign of the last days. So are famines, wars and earthquakes. Do not thank Jesus for the earthquake that just wiped out Guatemala or for those starving little black children in Ethiopia. In the same way, do not praise God for Israel, praise God that your name is written in the Lamb's Book of Life!

Give Israel the gospel. They are going to be deceived by the Antichrist and face the great tribulation. The seventieth week of Daniel is a reality. They *need* the gospel now more than ever, and thank God, they are getting it—but not from the Christian Zionists.

How shall they believe in Him whom they have not heard? And how shalt they hear without a preacher? (Romans 10:14).

This idea that all we have to do is show love, bless them socially, and then God will save the Jews, is not biblical. Do you know what dragged the Salvation Army down? They turned away from preaching the gospel as William Booth its founder had done, to social programs. Dr Bernardo was a man of God, if there ever was one. Three years ago Bernardo's in England abrogated the evangelical statement of faith. They do not preach the gospel to the kids any more.

I believe in social programs as a way of giving the gospel, but not in place of it. Social gospels are not the gospel of Jesus; they are only a trick. Yes, bless the poor, help the Jews, but give them the gospel! If they have no preacher, how shall they hear? The idea that we only need to bless them and bring them back and God will save them is unbiblical.

But it shall come about, if you will not obey the Lord your God, to observe to do all His commandments and His statutes with which I charge you today, that all these curses shall come upon you and overtake you. Cursed shall you be in the city, and cursed shall you be in the country... (Deut. 28:15-68).

And terrible things have happened to the Jews in the fulfilment of those curses: the scattering to the nations following the Bar Kochba rebellion (70 AD), the Spanish Inquisition, the Holocaust, the pogroms—these are the curse of the Law described in Leviticus 26 and Deuteronomy 28.

According to Romans, chapters one and two, because the gospel was first available to the Jews, the consequences for rejecting it are manifested against them first. The Law is either a blessing that points the people to the Messiah, or it is a curse that will judge them for rejecting Him (Deuteronomy 18:18-19). The Jews are under the curse of the Law. Only Jesus can break that curse, because He became a curse on the cross. Every Jew is under one covenant or another—either the Torah will point them to the Messiah, who fulfilled the Law, or they are under its curse.

So it shall be when all of these things have come upon you, the blessing and the curse which I have set before you, and you call them to mind in all nations where the Lord your God has banished you, and you return to the Lord your God and obey

Him with all your heart and soul according to all I command you today, you and your sons, then the Lord your God will restore you from captivity. (Deuteronomy 30:1–3).

The idea that we just bring the Jews back and then God will bring them to repentance is ridiculous. The opposite is true. Jews get saved in the Diaspora. How many Jews got saved under the communists in Russia? How many Jews are saved in the United States? There may be 100,000 Jewish born again Christians in North America. And more than 90 percent of them have been saved in the last fifteen to eighteen years. According to the American College of Rabbis, more Jews have embraced Christ in the last eighteen years, than in the last eighteen centuries. As the Torah said, the revival among the Jews would not begin in Israel, it would begin outside of it.

That is not to demean Jewish evangelism in Israel. I was an evangelist in Israel for years. I have been beaten up on the streets of Haifa. But I am telling you the truth. What the ICEJ are saying is just not biblical.

Those whom the devil cannot blind with error (like Replacement Theology and Cessationism), he will try to blind with Christian Zionism. Those who bring the most Jews back to Israel also bring them back to their Messiah. A love for the Jews that does not tell them about Jesus is *not* the love of Jesus. A burden for Jews that is not a burden for their salvation is *not* the burden of Christ!

Read what the Word of God says—Romans, chapters 9 to 11, is the reason why Arnold Fruchtenbaum and *Jews for Jesus* are so against the ICEJ; why the Lausanne Consultation on Jewish Evangelism said, "Withholding the gospel from the Jews is a form of anti-semitism;" and why Dr Harold Sevner, former president of the American Board of Missions to the Jews called the International Christian Embassy 'heretical' in the *Jerusalem Post*. I would not go that far because I know most of the people who are in the ICEJ are sincere. But what they are doing is not biblical. The ICEJ diverts millions of dollars away from the indigenous congregations in Israel and from Jewish evangelism to social programs in order to impress the rabbis and Israeli politicians.

These people are infatuated with diaspora Jewish culture. They are lifting up *Yiddishkeit* (Western European, Ashkenazi Jewish culture), not biblical Jewish culture. If they want to say there is something special about the fact that these Jews are growing up believing in their Messiah, despite the fact that their parents came through the holocaust, that would be one thing. But they do not marvel over my Jewish children accepting their Messiah, and the God of their fathers, they lift up *Yiddishkeit*.

They have become fascinated by Jewish schools and Jewish music. Let me tell you something, a lot of Jewish believers laugh at this stuff. They cannot help it. Some pro-Jewish believers are trying to be more Jewish than the Jews! Read Acts 15. You have your own culture. Do not be so ridiculous.

Now I can accept that people have done this out of ignorance. But once you have been told, it is no longer ignorance. God says, "I will require their blood at your hands."

It is the Jewish missions who preach Jesus that need your prayers. It is those who bring the Jews out of Russia *and* also share the gospel, like David and Jonathon and Beryl Hunter, who deserve your support. If you come across people who say, "We don't evangelise, we just love," they do not have the love of Jesus. Biblically, the only true embassy and ambassadors of Christ in Jerusalem are those who preach Him there and not those who do not (2 Corinthians 5:20).

I will bless those who bless you, and the one who curses you I will curse (Genesis 12:3). The best way you can bless a Jew, is to give them the gospel. Pray for their salvation and support those who witness to them. The worst way a born again Christian can curse a Jew is to withhold the gospel. If Yitshak Rabin could stand here right now in front of the ICEJ people, he would say, "You loved me? You loved me? Do you know where I am going to spend eternity because of your 'love'? Jesus was my Messiah. He died for me. He was one of my people, and you did not want to tell me about Him, because you 'loved' me?" Friends, that is not love!

When the *mo'el* [person specially trained to perform circumcision came to circumcise my son, I said the Hebrew prayers. The *mo'el* put some wine on cotton to give my son, and I asked him what the wine was for. He said, "To deaden the pain." Then he took out the circumcision knife, and I said, "If that kid could see the knife, he would say, 'Keep the wine, give me some Jack Daniels!'"

There is nothing special about Jews. There is something very special about the book of the Jews. There is something very special about the covenant with the Jews. There is something very special about the God of the Jews. There is something very special about the Messiah of the Jews. But the Jews are people who need their Messiah, just as much as Gentiles. I love Israel. I love the Jewish people. But I stand with Rabbi Sha'ul of Tarsus: *My heart's desire and my prayer to God for them is for their salvation* (Romans 10:1).

Dear friends, please do not participate in or support organisations that withhold the gospel from Jewish people. If you love the Jews, tell them about the King of the Jews.

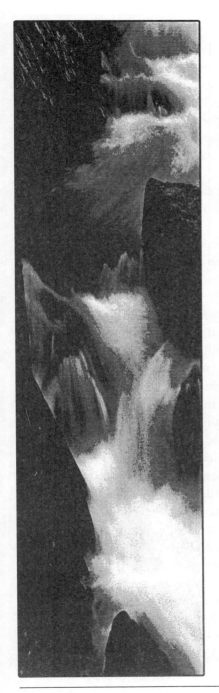

ELIJAH: A MAN WHO COULD MAKE IT RAIN

The effective prayer of a righteous man can accomplish much. Elijah was a man with a nature like ours, and he prayed earnestly that it might not rain; and it did not rain on the earth for three years and six months. And he prayed again, and the sky poured rain, and the earth produced its fruit (James 5:16-18).

ELIJAH was a man with a nature like ours. Elijah was a man who could make it rain. The Holy Spirit, through this text, is trying to tell us that, if he can do it, we can do it. We can make it rain. But what does that mean?

In biblical typology, different liquids again typify the Holy Spirit in different aspects. New wine is a liquid which represents the Holy Spirit in the aspect of worship. Another liquid is oil, which speaks of the anointing of the Holy Spirit. But the living water, in scripture, is always the Holy Spirit outpoured. The rain, outpoured, goes into the water table and becomes living water.

Jesus explained it this way: *"He who believes in Me, as the scripture said, "From his innermost being shall flow rivers of living water." But this He spoke of the Spirit whom those who believed in Him were to receive, for the Spirit was not yet given, because Jesus was not yet glorified* (John 7:38-39).

Jesus said directly that living water is the Holy Spirit outpoured.

For I will pour out water on the thirsty land and streams on the dry ground; I will pour out My Spirit on your offspring, and My blessing on your descendants (Isaiah 44:3).

Once again it says that God will pour out the water on the dry ground. And He says that this means He will pour out His Spirit. Rain is a figure of the Holy Spirit being poured out.

And furthermore, I withheld the rain from you while there were *still three months until harvest, Then I would send rain on one city and on another city I would not send rain; one part would be rained on, while the part not rained on would dry up* (Amos 4:7).

Why is it, for instance, that an evangelist can preach in Africa and see thousands and thousands of people saved at a single meeting, but if he goes to Germany or England or Australia, nothing much happens? The answer is here in Amos 4:7. God would send rain on one city, but on another city He would send no rain. And the city without the rain would have no harvest. This is a sovereign work of grace in the outpouring of His Spirit. It is raining in Brazil, Korea, Indonesia, Philippines and much of Africa. But in the western protestant countries which have had the bible for five hundred years, there is now a drought. God is turning His grace from the rich countries to the poor ones. White, protestant Christianity is in numerical, moral, theological and spiritual decline all over the world.

The church is growing in the Roman Catholic countries, the black countries, the olive skinned countries and the yellow skinned countries.

The Anglican Church has declined massively in England, yet most of the African Anglican bishops are outspoken evangelicals (Bishop Desmond Tutu being the notable exception). African Anglicans are terribly persecuted by Moslems in Nigeria. Throughout Asia the Anglican Church is very much alive. But in Britain, the Church of England is a dead church.

The old time fire that happened in the early days of pentecostalism such as the Sunshine revival in Australia, the Azusa Street revival in California and the Sunderland revivals in England with Smith Wigglesworth—that is what is happening now in places like Ecuador, Chile, the Philippines, Indonesia and Kenya.

God will send the rain on one city, while the city not rained on will dry up. Today we have people teaching formulas for church growth. That is nonsense. It does not work. There is a missing ingredient—the sovereign grace of God; His Spirit being outpoured.

His Word does not return void. Some people will be saved, one here and one there but, if you are talking about a massive harvest, no rain means no grain!

But Elijah was a man who could make it rain. And he was a man with a nature like ours. In other words, if he can do it, we can do it.

I am convinced that God wants to give the western protestant democracies one more chance to repent before Jesus comes. God wants to give the western countries another chance—not for our sake, but for His Name's sake. Not because we deserve it; we do not deserve it—our churches are, by and large, backslidden; but for the sake of our fathers.

As it says in Romans 11, God wants to give the Jews one more chance at the end of the world before Jesus comes. Why? Because when God looks at Israel, He does not just see Israel's sin and her ongoing rejection of her Messiah. When God looks at Israel, He still sees Jeremiah in prison, He still sees Isaiah being sawn in half by King Manasseh, He still sees Zachariah being martyred in the temple, He still sees John the Baptist having his head chopped off. And He says, "For the sake of their fathers, I want to give this nation one more chance."

Great Britain is the same. When God looks at Great Britain, He does not just see Britain as it is today—a so-called Christian country where Hindu gods are worshipped in Canterbury cathedral, while bishops deny the resurrection and the virgin birth.

When God looks at Britain today, He sees all of it—past, present and future. He still sees John Bunyan chained to the wall of the Bedford county jail for twelve years, and writing *The Pilgrim's Progress;* He still sees John Wesley being stoned by mobs who were stirred up by the Church of England for preaching the gospel; He still sees Tynedale being burned at a stake by the Church of Rome so we could have the bible in English; He still sees Charles Haddon Spurgeon; He still sees Ridley and Latimer and

Hooper; martyrs of England.

And God says, "For the sake of their fathers, and for My Name's sake, I want to give this nation one more chance."

That is equally true of the United States. He still sees Jonathon Edwards and D.L. Moody and Harry Ironsides. He sees the faithful Christians. He does not just see what we have today with the prosperity preachers the mammon worshippers and heretics.

God wants to give these western protestant nations one more chance to repent. But for them to have that chance, it has to rain. First of all, we have to face up to the fact that we are in a drought. And, until this drought ends, all the programs in the world will not bring about repentance and revival in the church. It takes rain.

No rain, no grain. No rain, no harvest.

Elijah was a man like us who could make it rain. And today, God is looking for men and women like us, who can make it rain.

Now Elijah the Tishbite, who was of the settlers of Gilead, said to Ahab, "the Lord, the God of Israel lives, before whom I stand, surely there shall be neither dew nor rain these years, except by my word."

And the word of the Lord came to him, saying, "Go away from here and turn eastward, and hide yourself by the brook Cherith, which is east of the Jordan. And it shall be that you shall drink of the brook, and I have commanded the ravens to provide for you there." So he did according to the word of the Lord, for he went and lived by the brook Cherith, which is east of the Jordan. And the ravens brought him bread and meat in the morning and bread and meat in the evening, and he would drink from the brook.

And it happened after a while, that the brook dried up, because there was no rain in the land. Then the word of the Lord came to him, saying, 'Arise, go to Zarephath, which belongs to Sidon, and stay there; behold, I have commanded a widow there to provide for you.'

So he arose and went to Zarephath, and when he came to the gate of the city, behold, a widow was there gathering sticks; and he called to her and said, "Please get me a little water in a jar, that I may drink."

And as she was going to get it, he called to her and said, "Please bring me a piece of bread in your hand."

But she said, "As the Lord your God lives, I have no bread, only a handful of flour in the bowl and a little oil in the jar; and behold, I am gathering a few sticks that I may go in and prepare for me and my son, that we may eat it and die."

Then Elijah said to her, "Do not fear; go, do as you have said, but make me a little bread cake from it first, and bring it out to me, and afterward you may make one for yourself and for your son.

"For thus says the Lord God of Israel, 'The bowl of flour shall not be exhausted, nor shall the jar of oil be empty until the day that the Lord sends rain on the face of the earth'".

So she went and did according to the word of Elijah, and she and he and her household ate for many days.

The bowl of flour was not exhausted nor did the jar of oil become empty according to the word of the Lord which He spoke through Elijah. Now it came about after these things, that the son of the woman, the mistress of the house, became sick; and his sickness was so severe, that there was no breath left in him.

So she said to Elijah, "What have I to do with you, O man of God? You have come to me to bring my iniquity to remembrance, and to put my son to death!"

And he said to her, "Give me your son." Then he took him from her bosom and carried him up to the upper room where he was living, and laid him on his own bed. And he called to the Lord and said, "O Lord God, hast Thou also brought calamity to the widow with whom I am staying, by causing her son to die?"

Then he stretched himself upon the child three times, and called to the Lord, and said, "O Lord my God, I pray Thee, let this child's life return to him."

And the Lord heard the voice of Elijah, and the life of the child returned to him and he revived. And Elijah took the child, and brought him down from the upper room into the house and gave him to his mother; and Elijah said, "See, your son is alive".

Then the woman said to Elijah, "Now I know you are a man of God, and that the word of the Lord in your mouth is truth."

Now it came about after many days, that the word of the Lord came to Elijah in the third year, saying, "Go, show yourself to Ahab, and I will send rain on the face of the earth."

So Elijah went to show himself to Ahab. Now the famine was severe in Samaria (1 Kings 17:1-18:2).

And it came about, when Ahab saw Elijah that Ahab said to him, "Is this you, you troubler of Israel?" (1 Kings 18:17).

Then Elijah said to them, "Seize the prophets of Baal; do not let one of them escape." So they seized them; and Elijah brought them down to the brook Kishon, *and slew them there.*

Now Elijah said to Ahab, "Go up, eat and drink for there is the sound of the roar of a heavy shower."

So Ahab went up to eat and drink. But Elijah went up to the top of Carmel; and he crouched down on the earth, and put his face between his knees. And he said to his servant, "Go up now, look toward the sea." So he went up and looked and said, "There is nothing." And he said, "Go back" seven times. And it came about at the seventh time, that he said "Behold, a cloud as small as a man's hand is coming up from the sea." And he said, "Go up, say to Ahab 'Prepare your chariot and go down, so that the heavy shower does not stop you.'"

So it came about in a little while, that the sky grew black with clouds and there was a heavy shower. And Ahab rode and went to Jezreel. Then the hand of the Lord was on Elijah, and he girded up his loins and outran Ahab to Jezreel (1 Kings 18:40-46).

And it rained and it rained and it rained.

The three and a half years in which it did not rain in the story of Elijah is a type of the three and a half years referred to in Daniel and Revelation, when the Spirit will not be outpoured at the end of the world. It is a type of what happens eschatologically, when the spirit of Elijah comes back into operation in some way, as predicted by the prophet Malachi. Similarly, the way that Elijah rescued the Gentile woman and her son teaches something about the way that God is going to use the spirit of Elijah, somehow, to take care of the Gentile church at the end of the world.

Elijah, Elisha and John the Baptist all had the same spirit. The Lord told Moses that He would *"take of the Spirit who is upon you, and will put Him upon the elders of the people"* (Numbers 11:17). When events happen in the same geographical location it usually means that there is some spiritual and theological connection between them. Elijah's ministry ended on the plain of Jericho, where Elisha received his mantle (meaning his authority), and John the Baptist's ministry occurred in the same place.

The wicked woman, Jezebel, is a type of the woman Jezebel in the Book of Revelation—the spirit of false religion—who turned the king, the political power, into someone she could manipulate. On behalf of Ahab, she obtained Naboth's vineyard, which Ahab coveted.

In scripture, the vineyard speaks of Israel and, by extension or incorporation, the church. The wicked woman tried to get the vineyard for the king. This brought her into conflict with Elijah and she persuaded the king to try to destroy Elijah. This is exactly the picture in the story of Herodias (Matthew 14:3-12)—the wicked woman who turned the king against Elijah (John the Baptist).

Wicked women in the bible all point in some way to the character of the wicked woman in the book of Revelation, where the conflict with Elijah is going be replayed in the last days.

The first thing in our study of how God takes a man like Elijah and turns him into someone who can make it rain is to learn why the rain stopped.

The rain stopped because of the sin of God's people. The Holy Spirit is not being outpoured on the western protestant world because of its sin, which is identical to the sin of Israel in the days of Elijah.

Abortion replays the sacrifice of children to demons that we see among Israel and Judah in the Old Testament.

The worship of other gods. The priests of Baal were not foreigners, they were Jews. Today it is the same. Across the western protestant world there is a dramatic increase in the worship of other gods—Islam, New Age, Hinduism. New Age is permeating many of the evangelical and Pentecostal churches today. People are mixing Christianity with paganism—that is where Roman Catholicism came from and that is what is happening today in many Pentecostal churches.

Materialism. The church is lukewarm, materialistic, filled with crazy doctrines. It has a version of "faith" that is not biblical—the worship of mammon in Christian masquerade; covetousness disguised as Christianity.

That is why the rain stopped. The first and foremost responsibility for the decline of western civilisation does not lie with secular society, it lies with us. It was, the sin of God's people that stopped the rain. The problems proliferating throughout our society—drugs, abortion, divorce, violence, crime—all testify to the failure of the church.

God's people compromised and eventually Israel ended up with the priests of Baal. That is what happened in Elijah's day and that is what is going on today. It is not raining in our countries because of the sin of God's people.

The first thing God told Elijah to do was to go to *the brook Cherith, which is east of the Jordan* (1 Kings 17:3), and there the ravens would feed him. Cherith was on the other side of the Jordan. When God told Elijah to leave his land and go to Cherith; He told him to leave behind his national identity, his cultural identity and his religious identity. On top of that, Elijah was to be fed by ravens. Ravens were not kosher, they were an "unclean" bird. God was going to provide for him in ways he would never have expected.

The drought is so critical in the western world today that people who would make it rain will have to be willing to go to Cherith. Sometimes that will mean churches leaving traditional denominations that have compromised. Sometimes that will mean Christians leaving churches that have compromised or that have gone into error and refuse to repent. And it will certainly mean trusting God to meet your needs in ways and in places you might not expect, even through things we consider to be almost unholy, like the ravens.

Elijah had to be willing to put God first and his land second.

So often today, the problem is that people are putting their land first their culture, their identity, their denominations and their loyalties to those denominations—before obedience to the Word of God. But the people who will make it rain will be people who are not afraid to go to Cherith and trust God.

It is darkest before the dawn. Things will become much worse before they get better. The brook of Cherith will eventually dry up. In verse 9, we see that Elijah has to go to a place called *Zarephath*. The word *Zarephath* comes from the Hebrew infinitive meaning 'to burn' or 'to purify by fire'.

For God to take somebody with a nature like ours and turn them into somebody who can make it rain, He needs to purify them by fire.

There is going to be a very difficult period—not just trial and testing, not just drought, nor even persecution—but all those things together. It will get to the point where the people you try to help will think you have betrayed them, as with the widow at Zarephath. But no matter how bad things get, no matter how dark it becomes, no matter how critical the drought, I can promise you two things: there will be flour in the dish and oil in the jar for those who are willing to be purified. Things are going to get bad before the breakthrough comes. But there is going to be flour in the dish and oil in the jar. You will have the Word of God and you will have the anointing of the Spirit, no matter what happens. You will have your grain and your oil when the others die from famine.

So she said to Elijah, "What have I to do with you, O man of God? You have come to me to bring my iniquity to remembrance, and to put my son to death!" (1 Kings 17:18).

Her son died. And she blamed Elijah. The very people you try to help will see the hardship and they will blame you.

Things have been so bad for so long, that the things we love most will have to die before they can be resurrected. Much of the church in the western world will have to die before it can be resurrected. New wine cannot go into old wine skins. That was one of the problems with the charismatic movement; they tried to store the new wine in the old wine skins. In order to renew a church you have to replace the wine skin. The things that we have loved the most will have to die before they can be resurrected.

"Is this you, you troubler of Israel?" (1Kings 18:17).

Is this you, you troubler of the church? Is this you, you troubler of the Baptist Union? Is this you, you troubler of the Assemblies of God?

You who are standing up against ecumenism and Kingdom Now and faith prosperity and name-it-and-claim-it. You who are standing up against false miracles and bogus healings. You who are standing up against ministers making themselves rich by exploiting pensioners with lies. You troublers of Israel!

That is what they said to Elijah and, if you want to make it rain, that is what they are going to say to you.

Next they go to Mount Carmel. Here the conflict occurs with Jezebel; the conflict with the spirit of false religion, with Roman Catholicism, ecumenism, Freemasonry, Islam, homosexuality and New Age. There is going to be a conflict, and those who win that conflict will be those who have been purified at Zarephath.

So much of what we call "charismatic worship" today with the noise, the ranting and raving, and the hype, looks more like the priests of Baal on Mount Carmel than like Elijah.

Notice that the priests of Baal really thought it would work, they thought they would get a response. Our brethren today, caught up in ecumenism, Kingdom Now theology, Restorationism all unbiblical, false and dangerous doctrines; all associated with hype and with prophecies that do not happen—actually believe these things. But the conflict will come and the people will see who the true prophets are.

It begins small. It does not seem like any thing is going to happen at first. Where is it? With the priests of Baal it was all loud boasting and arrogance, and cheering, and hype. But God does not work that way. It begins small; like a little hand coming out of the sea. It always begins small. But it gets bigger and soon the whole sky is filled with rain clouds. Lightning strikes and God's Spirit falls. And it rains and rains and rains.

There is no easy way to stop the decline of Christianity in the western world. It has gone too far for too long. We have been sold down the river by our leaders. All the programs and hype and gimmicks in the world will not bring a harvest of souls. That takes rain. But the rain has stopped.

Why? Partly because of the sin of society, but mostly because of the sin of the church. And until there is a repentance in the church, there is not going to be a repentance in the world.

Why has the rain stopped? It is not primarily the fault of pornographers or pimps or prostitutes or drug dealers or homosexuals or abortionists. It is primarily my fault, because I have the gospel. It is my fault, because I have the Holy Spirit. It is my fault, because I know the truth and I have the message that can make the difference.

It is our fault, because the church in the west is Laodicea (Revelation 3:17); because we are lukewarm Christians; because we are trusting in this life and this world more than we are trusting in Jesus. It is not raining because of my sin and your sin.

Those who make it rain will be those who are not afraid to go to *Cherith* - people who are not bound by tradition or institutions. They will not try to put new wine in old wine skins. They will do what God tells them and trust God to provide for them in ways they do not expect.

They will be people who are not afraid to be purified, people who will go to *Zarephath,* people who are willing to see things that they love die, knowing that those things will be resurrected in purity.

It will be difficult. But no matter how difficult it gets, I promise you that there will be oil in the jar and flour in the dish.

And those people who are purified will go to *Carmel* and stand in front of Jezebel—in front of false religion and Freemasonry and homosexuality and Roman Catholicism and Islam. They will stand in front of the prophets of Baal—those who dare to call themselves ministers of the gospel, but who compromise with false teaching. There will be a conflict. And those troublers of Israel are going to win.

CURSES AND CHRISTIANS

T HE early church had something that many of us today have lost. And when I say "us," I mean people like me: people who believe in the gifts of the Spirit.

Now these were more noble-minded than those in Thessalonica, for they received the word with great eagerness, examining the scriptures daily to see whether these things were so (Acts 17).

We have something in churches today that comes from the secular world and the false religious systems—a 'guru' mentality. Whatever the Brahman priest says, that is what his followers or devotees will believe. Whatever the guru says, his devotees will follow. Roman Catholics will believe the teachings of the Pope, simply because he is the Pope and with no reference to anything else, other than the Pope said it. Orthodox Jews will believe whatever the rabbis tell them, particularly Hassidic Jews. He goes to God directly through the Torah; you go to God through him. Moslems go to the Imam. He goes to directly to Allah; you go through him.

This mentality has come into the body of Christ like an avalanche in the last thirty years, particularly in the last ten. A mindset has developed among Christians whereby anyone who is plainly called and gifted of God now has their word treated as if it were the Word of God, without any sense of a need to check it out. If he said it, that's it!

Paul did miracles, signs and wonders; he saw healings and tremendous conversions. Whole churches were planted. He wrote half of the New Testament. He was a rabbi of the rabbis, a pharisee from the school of Hillel. He was a disciple of Rabbi Gamaliel. Imagine if a famous rabbi gave his life to Jesus and began doing miracles today; people would make him into a guru and whatever he said, that would be it.

But Paul never claimed to be a guru. What did he say? *But even though we, or an angel from heaven, should preach to you a gospel contrary to that which we have preached to you, let him be accursed* (Galatians 1:8).

What made a man like Paul great was that he always realized that the real authority came from Jesus and God's word. He was a good steward of the authority vested in him. There are people today whom God has called and blessed with gifts like miracles and healings, whom God uses and through whom many are saved, but a mentality has come into the church whereby whatever that person says becomes *the* truth. Full stop. We make them into gurus. It is not only Jews, Catholics, Hindus and Mormons, but Christians are doing so, particularly in Restorationism and the house churches.

The Greek word for *heresy* does not simply mean doctrinal error. The real meaning refers to someone who is hyper-schismatic, someone who forms a faction. The book of Galatians speaks directly to the sin of 'party spirit.' Party spirit does not mean we are all going to a bar to have joints and a beer. Party spirit means you form a league, not of God's Spirit, which claims to have a corner on truth. Everyone outside the group is a second rate believer, or second rate Christian.

The only real basis of truth is the bible. In the best churches you are going to find some wrong things and some wrong people; and in the bad churches, you are going to find some right things and some right people. Look at the seven churches in Revelation.

Party spirit, or a tendency to form factions, is a 'deed of the flesh'

(Galatians 5:19-21). Denominations are one thing, but denominationalism is simply a euphemism for the sin of party spirit. I am not against forming an association as a practical mechanism to get churches working together in things like missions, evangelism, and helping the poor. But when people begin forming a league, cutting themselves off from the Body of Christ, that is different. There are two kinds of division. The bible says there will be factions among you to prove what is true. Ecumenism, of course, is a unity not of God's Spirit, it is a false unity.

The Holy Spirit is the Spirit of Truth. You cannot build the unity of the Spirit on error. To unite with churches that teach salvation comes through 'sacraments,' instead of by being born again and that practice transubstantiation and praying to the dead, is flagrantly immoral. That is not the unity of the Spirit. Bible believing Christians cannot unite with the false religious system of this world.

On the other hand, it is totally wrong for bible believing Christians and churches to be inordinately divided from each other.

I am not saying there should be some kind of a monolithic organisation, but there should be a unity of the Spirit, based on a common experience of God's grace and salvation in Jesus, and commitment to the authority of His word.

People tend to get hold of a doctrine, amplify that doctrinal truth, and make it into some kind of colossal issue and build a church around it. But truth becomes a lie when people make that truth the basis for all other truths.

The one biblical basis for all truth is Jesus. Christ died; Christ rose from the dead; Christ is coming again. The cross, the empty tomb, and the Mount of Olives—that is the basic truth upon which all other truths must be built. All other truths must be centrally predicated on the truth of Jesus.

After centuries in which the truth of the Holy Spirit was suppressed by both Catholics and Protestants, along came charismatics and pentecostals who got hold of this truth and made it into the basis for all other truth. They wound up with a very distorted, unbiblical picture of the Holy Spirit.

The ministry of the Holy Spirit is pictured for us in, Abraham sending his servant to get a bride for his son Isaac. Isaac the son corresponds to Jesus. Abraham corresponds to the Father. The servant is the Holy Spirit.

The Father sent his Servant to prepare a bride for His Son, from amongst His own people. The Holy Spirit is always a servant who points people to Jesus.

When the Holy Spirit is amplified above Jesus, we see people singing "Come Holy Spirit." The Holy Spirit is never prayed to in the bible. He is only worshipped in the context of the triunity of the godhead, as part of the trinity, but He is never prayed to directly.

So a truth becomes a lie. Instead of Jesus being the central truth upon which all other truth is based, another truth is put in the place of Jesus. Even though it is a truth, it becomes virtually false. And with this false teaching comes all kinds of charismatic excesses and crazy doctrine.

Another is the truth of curses: there is a biblical truth about curses, but I see people obsessed with it. I have been in churches where the whole emphasis of the ministry is "casting demons out of Christians," and breaking curses. They talk more about the devil than they do about Jesus. Every problem, supposedly, has something to do with a curse or a demon. Much of this is due to people not wanting to take personal responsibility for their own relationship with Jesus. Again, it is the guru mentality.

We live in a specialist society. If I have a legal problem, I phone my lawyer. If I have a medical problem, I phone my doctor. If I have a financial problem, I call my banker. If I have a spiritual problem, I phone the preacher. He is the professional, he is the guru. What pill should I take doctor? What legal action should I take, lawyer? What should I do, preacher?

Among people like myself who believe in the gifts of the Spirit, there is a deficiency of scholarly people. We lack gifted teachers. Most of our preachers are ignorant of doctrine. Very few have any knowledge of academic theology or any real confidence in Greek or Hebrew. The bible says, "My people perish for a lack of knowledge," and people today are perishing for a lack of knowledge. For that reason I had developed tremendous respect for Derek Prince. Derek Prince is one of the few charismatic bible teachers who really studies the Word, who will go to the trouble to look at the original languages, to become functionally competent in lexical exegesis.

He takes these things and uses them to meet people's practical needs. I have only spoken to him twice, but I have always respected him and his ministry, I would estimate that 90 percent of what Derek Prince teaches is very good to excellent. It would be a tremendous tragedy if people were ever to throw the baby out with the bath water.

It is a tragedy that Derek Prince fell for the Pentecostal deception; that he has compromised on the issue of Roman Catholicism, has in the past toyed with prosperity doctrine and shepherding—but most troubling is his dangerously wrong teaching on curses and deliverances.

There are two dangers. One danger is people will find something which they see is wrong, or God shows them it is wrong and they will reject the entire ministry on that basis. Unless there is something fundamentally wrong, affecting the gospel itself, such as Copeland, Kenyon, and Hagin saying that "Jesus died spiritually, it was not finished on the cross," we should be pretty hesitant to reject everything someone says on the basis of one or two errors, or a small percentage of it. None of us are perfect. I certainly am not perfect.

There are four criteria that give us authority to reject someone's ministry completely.

1. Immorality: Unconfessed sins, ongoing, unrepentant immorality— that is a reason to reject someone's ministry.

2. The Gospel: If someone replaces the gospel with another way of salvation—based on works, based on the law, based on sacraments they are to be rejected. The bible teaches the priesthood of all believers. The Roman Catholic church, Eastern Orthodox churches and Mormon church all put back a special priesthood, denying the new covenant as the New Testament teaches it.

3. The Person of Christ. What do they believe about Jesus? Is He the Way, the Truth and the Life? When someone believes and teaches something unorthodox about Jesus, reject it and them.

4. The Authority of Scripture. When they replace the authority of scripture with some other basis of doctrinal authority, based on some other 'revelation,' reject it.

Restorationism is mostly gnosticism, subjective revelation. Instead of exegesis, they practice eisegesis—reading into the Word something that is not there.

Roman Catholicism says that the teaching of the church is more important than the Word of God; what the church says about the bible is what counts. *My soul exalts the Lord, and my spirit has rejoiced in God my*

Saviour (Luke 1:46-47). Mary said she needs a saviour, but the Pope can say, "No, she was conceived without sin, she does not." Who are you going to believe?

If there is immorality, rejection of the authority of scripture or the person of Jesus, or another gospel, you can reject the whole thing.

I believe the main problem is with us. We have lost the spirit of the Bereans. We will take on board something that somebody says, simply because they seem so right most of the time.

Let not many of you become teachers, my brethren, knowing that as such we shall incur a stricter judgment (James 3:1).

I do not want to teach the bible. I would rather be an evangelist and leave this kind of thing to others. I only do it because the Holy Spirit has shown me, largely through other people around the world, that this is what He wants me to concentrate on. If it was up to me, I would rather be out there reaching the lost. I know that God is going to hold me more accountable than he holds you.

The lamp of your body is your eye; when your eye is clear, your whole body also is full of light; but when it is bad, your body also is full of darkness. Then watch out that the light in you may not be darkness (Luke 11-35). This is a midrash on human anatomy, with the human eye standing for the teacher.

Never take what I say on face value. I am going to be accountable to God for what I teach you. Please, I have enough to give account for. Be like the Bereans, take what I say before the Lord and test it. Do not make me a guru. Do not make people like Derek Prince and others into gurus either. God bless and use these people, but for their sake, as well as your own, do not make them into your guru.

The first mistake made by people who teach about blessings and cursings, and who say that Christians can be accursed, is that they do not look at the original Hebrew and Greek, or consider the context in which the words are used. When you do this you can see the ways in which Christians can be cursed and the ways in which they cannot be cursed.

There are different words in Hebrew and Greek for curses, words that are not always interchangeable, but mostly used in specific ways.

One complication in scholarship is that the New Testament takes Hebrew concepts and translates them into Greek. We need to go to the ancient Septuagint and see how the rabbis understood the Hebrew when they translated it into Greek. Sometimes there are different Greek words for something in Hebrew where there is only one word. In Hebrew there is only one word for 'love,' *ahovah,* but in Greek there is no less than seven words for 'love'—three, possibly four, of which occur in the bible (three are stated, and the fourth is implied without being stated).

When you begin looking at the different words in the original languages, trying to see the context in which they are used, various kinds of problems arise. Nonetheless, we can learn how people, even Christians, can in some ways be cursed, and also how they cannot.

One way to understand what a word or a concept means in Hebraic or Jewish thought is to understand the word opposite. If you know what 'cold' means, you can understand what 'hot' means. If you know what 'convex' means, you will have an idea of what 'concave' means. Hebrew is like that, it is structured in terms of antithesis. If you understand the antithesis of something, that will help you understand what the word means.

1. Kelolah

The first word for 'curse' is *kelolah,* meaning "imprecation—praying evil or misfortune on someone." It is the opposite of being blessed. When good things happen it is *berakah,* 'a blessing'. The agricultural cycle in Israel is dependent upon the rain. When it rains, even though the rain might come very heavily, causing flash floods, the people say the rain is a blessing.

Lack of rain is seen as a curse. Israel was required to live by faith. The rain was a sign of God's blessing. When the rain was withheld, it was seen as a sign of his disfavour. *For I will pour out water on the thirsty land and streams on the dry ground; I will pour out My Spirit on your offspring, and My blessing on your descendants* (Isaiah 44:3).

As we have seen, different liquids typify or represent the Holy Spirit in different aspects of His ministry. In worship and the joy of worship, it is the new wine that represents the Holy Spirit. For anointing, it is oil. For his Spirit outpoured, it is living water, the fresh clean rain water that goes into the cisterns. The bible refers to 'living water' in Isaiah 44, and in Jeremiah. Jesus draws on it in John 7. This rain represents the outpouring of the Holy Spirit. The rain caused the harvest. If there was no rain, there would be no grain. It is the same today. If there is no rain, there is no grain, and there is no harvest. There is a famine for hearing the word of God. There is a potential harvest of souls that is not being reaped. There is no crop.

The main biblical emphasis of the concept of *kelolah* lies not with people, but with nations being accursed or blessed. It is less personal and has more to do with a corporate blessing or curse.

And furthermore, I withheld the rain from you while there was still three months until harvest. Then I would send rain on one city and on another city I would not send rain; one part would be rained on, while the part not rained on would dry up (Amos 4:7).

When an honest evangelist who preaches the honest gospel—not amplifying healings above repentance or squeezing the people for money—goes to Africa, literally tens of thousands of people will give their lives to Jesus in just one crusade. Sometimes in just one meeting. Why? Because the rain is being outpoured, the Holy Spirit is being outpoured, in Africa. That same evangelist with the same gifting and same anointing can go to England or to some other European country and practically nothing in comparison will happen.

The gifting can be there. The anointing can be there. The rain is being withheld. This land is accursed, there is *kelolah*.

The spiritual destitution you see in Britain today—the neo-paganism, the church being a dead middle-class institution, the fundamental breakdown of the moral fabric of this society, the disintegration of family values, all of it—is due to this nation being accursed.

Great Britain is not being blessed, it is being cursed. In 1951 they had the third biggest economy in the world. Great Britain cannot even compete with Italy or France any more, let alone Germany or Japan. The economic and political decline of Great Britain is a reflection of its spiritual decline. It is accursed.

But if you do not obey Me... those who hate you shall rule over you (Leviticus 26:14-17).

In the year 2010—and I am being careful to keep my political views separate from my biblical views—it is a fact that in the year 2010 at least 80 percent of Great Britain's laws will be made, not by their own elected parliament, but by bankers and bureaucrats in Brussels, in Frankfurt at the Central Bank, and in Germany.

By 2010 Great Britain will be governed by people they did not vote for and who they cannot remove.

That is already happening in Britain and America is not far behind. There is a curse on Britain, and America is running close behind in—the same direction.

The sign of that curse is the fact that the Holy Spirit is not being rained upon those nations. There is no harvest taking place. Even big events like Billy Graham crusades—well organised, well financed meetings—do nothing to even turn the church around, let alone the country. But if you go to Ghana, Brazil, Korea, people cannot believe the growth. Why? Because it is raining in those countries.

2. Me'airoh

The next word is *me'airoh,* which means bitterness—not imprecation (an invoking of evil), but execration (a detesting, loathing, abhorrence), an expression of hatred. It is the opposite of 'love.'

To understand the Hebraic thought patterns and world view that God worked through to produce the Old Testament and the New Testament (partly), you have to understand the principle of opposites. To know what something means, you have to understand its opposite. The idea here is that you curse someone by not loving them. Love will break this kind of curse. Can Christians come under this kind of a curse? Yes, they can.

Jesus said, *The world hates you, you know that it has hated Me before it hated you. If you were of the world, the world would love its own; but because you are not of the world, but I chose you out of the world, therefore the world hates you* (John 15:18-19).

I know Christian women who have unsaved husbands who hate them. I know Jewish people who got saved, their families hate them; their families do not love them, they hate them. Yes, Christians can be under this kind of a curse. We are all under this kind of a curse.

The whole world lies in the power of the evil one (1 John 5:19).

Jesus said the world hates you. In this sense, Christians can be under a curse.

3. Kalal

And it will come about that just as you were a curse among the nations, O house of Judah and house of Israel, so will I save you that you may become a blessing. Do not fear; let your hands be strong (Zechariah 8:13).

This word *kalal* comes from the Hebrew word *kal* meaning 'light' (as in not heavy). The Hebrew word for 'heavy' is *kaved,* it is the same word for 'liver' (the largest organ of a body of a human), or 'large mammal'.

The word for 'honour' in Hebrew is *kavod,* which is drawn from *kovaid,* 'heavy.' The Hebrew principle of opposites applies here. The opposite of 'to curse' is 'to honour.' If you honour someone or something, it has weight; it is heavy for you. If something is dishonoured, it is cursed; it is of lightweight consideration to you. Something can be light or it can be heavy.

The Hebrew idea of "honouring your parents" really means that they should be something heavy for you. If someone is heavy for you, it means something. If a political figure made a comment in the newspaper that you did not like, that would be light for you. You do not have much respect for that person. If you were reading the bible, and the Holy Spirit convicted you of something, or showed you something in scripture, that would be heavy for you.

The opposite of *kalal,* light, is *kaved,* heavy, leading to *kavod,* practical honour and respect.

In this sense, Christians can be cursed and also curse others. If we are considered lightly by other people, instead of being seen as God's new creation, it is a form of being cursed. But if we do not let other believers and our parents, in particular, be heavy for us, we are cursing them.

In its practical outworking, this idea has to do with responsibility. We are held accountable in God's design for the welfare of our parents in their old age. Maybe we are concerned for other older people, or elderly, or retired people. Our own parents should be heavy for us. If we are neglecting our responsibility for the financial well-being of our parents, we are cursing them. The idea in the bible of cursing your parents which is worthy of death in the Old Testament and also a very serious sin in the New Testament—is letting them be light for you instead of heavy. My family is a combination of Irish Catholic, and Jewish. I cannot be in the room with my mother for five minutes without arguing if we begin talking about the bible. The woman drives me nuts. Having a mother like that prepared me for my wife. I do not like my mother's ideas too much and we do not get along particularly well. But she is still heavy for me. Every time I think about her, I pray, "Lord Jesus, please save my mother. Don't let her die and go to hell, like my father did. Please, she is heavy for me."

My mother is reasonably well off financially. If she wasn't, it would be my responsibility to take care of her.

If I did not do that, I would be cursing her because she would be 'light' instead of 'heavy' for me. In this sense, Christians can be cursed.

4. Cherem

Cherem means that some thing has been devoted to a bad fate.

And He will restore the hearts of the fathers to their children, and the hearts of the children to their fathers [speaking of the ministry of Elijah], *lest I come and smite the land with a curse* (Malachi 4:6).

This idea of smiting the land with a curse means devoting it to destruction; it becomes a determined purpose of God to give something over to being ruined. This world is fallen and under a cherem, under a curse. *For we know that the whole creation groans and suffers the pains of childbirth together until now* (Romans 8:22).

Natural disasters—bushfires, volcanic eruptions, earthquakes, famines, droughts—these things are all byproducts of the fall of man. God gave man dominion over creation. When man fell, the creation fell with him. There were certain changes in geology, physics, meteorology, biology, and so on. We live in a cursed world. Not merely in a fallen world, but in a cursed one. In this sense, Christians can be cursed.

However, Egypt was devoted to God's judgment because Egypt would not let God's people go. But when these judgments were poured out on Egypt—events which we commemorate in Passover—God's people were preserved in them and through them. We are preserved in and through the curse, but we are still under the curse. In all of these senses, a Christian can be cursed.

5. Katara

Hebrews is an important book for understanding the Jewish thought of the early church because it was written to Jewish Christians.

For ground that drinks the rain which often falls upon it and brings forth vegetation useful to those for whose sake it is also tilled, receives a blessing from God (Hebrews 6:7).

Do you see how the New Testament recycles the teaching of Isaiah 44 and Amos 4 about the rain being a blessing? It uses the physical agriculture, physical meteorology, to teach us about the outpouring of the Spirit.

But if it yields thorns and thistles, it is worthless and close to being cursed, and it ends up being burned (Hebrews 6:8).

That is what happens in a fallen world. The New Testament recycles this concept in the word *katara*, 'cursed.' In the same way that the creation is under a curse, this curse can come upon Christians, just because they are in a fallen world.

But, beloved, we are convinced of better things concerning you, and things that accompany salvation, though we are speaking in this way; For God is not unjust so as to forget your work and the love which you have shown towards His name, in having ministered and in still ministering to the saints (Hebrews 6:9-10).

The idea is that even though the creation is cursed, and even though you are subject to this curse, God will see you through it and deliver you out of it. However, see what precedes this word *katara*.

For in the case of those who have once been enlightened and have tasted of the heavenly gift and have been made partakers of the Holy Spirit, and have tasted the good word of God and the powers of the age to come [These are people who were saved], *and then have fallen away* [In the Greek there is no present tense, but a present continual tense—those who are actively backsliding to the point that they are not going to come back], *it is impossible to renew them again unto repentance, since they again crucify to themselves the Son of God, and put Him to open shame. For the ground...* and it goes on to talk about the rain and the curse on the land (Hebrews 6:4-7).

It is only in Jesus that we can be saved from the curse and ultimately delivered out of it. When you fall away from Jesus, you put yourself back under the curse in its fullest sense. You go back and, instead of harvesting vegetables, you are going to harvest thorns. In that sense a backslidden Christian can be cursed.

Then He will also say to those on his left, "Depart from Me, accursed ones, into the eternal fire which has been prepared for the devil and his angels" (Matthew 25:41). The same Greek word, *katara* is used here. Backsliders put themselves back under the curse of hell.

6. Katal

There is another Hebrew word, *katal* which means 'to call down evil.'

A Christian can have evil called down upon them. I would not dispute that the blood of Jesus and His divine intervention can protect us from it, but to say that we are going to be immune from it is unscriptural.

The pagan Roman emperors called down a curse on the church and persecuted Christians, who went to their deaths as martyrs. We can certainly be cursed in this sense.

However, God says, "I will bless them that bless thee, and curse them that curse thee." During the Second World War the Nazis built a wall around the Jewish ghetto. Any Jew trying to escape the ghetto by climbing over the wall was machine gunned.

A few years later, a wall went up around the once glorious capital of the Reich, Berlin, and any German caught climbing over the wall was machine gunned. This continued for almost fifty years, until that generation of German leaders was dead. "I will bless them that bless thee, and curse them that curse thee."

Countries like Denmark and Holland have a staggering level of immorality. The pornography in Denmark and the drugs and sexual sin in Holland is horrible. One of the reasons, possibly the main reason, that God has not judged those countries so far is that when the Nazis said all the Jews had to come out and wear a yellow star, many of the people of Denmark and Holland came out and said, "Jesus was a Jew, and so am I. Here's my star."

In the Roman Catholic countries, like Poland and France, the people helped the Nazis to kill the Jews.

In the protestant countries with the high evangelical population, like Denmark and Holland, the people protected the Jews, sometimes at the expense of their own lives. Think of people like Corrie Ten Boom.

God said, *"I will bless them that bless thee and curse them that curse thee."* This is a dynamic and active principle.

7. Anathematizo

But he began to curse and swear, "I do not know this man you are talking about!" (Mark 14:71).

The Greek word *anathematizo* means 'to say bad things in anger.' Can Christians be cursed in this sense? Of course they can.

8. Katanathematizo

Closely related to *anathematizo* is the word *katanathematizo*, which means 'to betray a loved one.'

Brother will deliver up brother to death, and a father his child; and children will rise up against parents, and cause them to be put to death (Matthew 10:21).

Christians will betray one another, particularly in the last days; Jesus said so. And, yes, we can also be cursed in this manner in times of persecution.

We have looked at all the ways that the bible says believers can be cursed. Now let us look at how they cannot be cursed.

For as many as are of the works of the law are under a curse; for it is written, "Cursed is everyone who does not abide by all things written in the book of the law, to perform them."

Now that no one is justified by the Law before God is evident; for, "The righteous man shall live by faith."

However, the Law is not of faith; on the contrary, "He who practices them shall live by them" (Galatians 3:10–12).

The main purpose of the law was to teach the Jews that they could not keep the law, that they could never reach up to God's standard. They needed a Messiah to save them. It is only in Jesus that we can keep the law, because He has fulfilled it for us.

Suppose you were fined $30 million and could not pay the fine, but a multi-millionaire wrote out a cheque for you. He would be doing something for you that you could not possibly do for yourself. Jesus has done that for us.

When you have a religion that puts you back under the law, it sets up a standard you could never live up to. Jesus said, *"I say to you, among those born of women, there is no one greater than John; yet he who is least in the kingdom of God is greater than he"* (Luke 7:28).

Why? John the Baptist represents the ultimate standard or level of righteousness, capable of being achieved by good works. He was the ultimate; no religious person was any better or more religious in their standard of behaviour than John. He was a unique man, filled with the Holy Spirit from his mothers womb (Luke 1:15).

What the ancient Jewish heresy of Ebionism falsely believed about Jesus—that he was a uniquely inspired man—was in fact true about John the Baptist. John is the most unique man who ever lived, apart from Jesus, with the possible exception of Adam. Yet he who is least in the kingdom of God, is greater than John. Why? Anybody who is born again, who has the righteousness of Jesus—who fulfilled the Law—is greater than any righteousness we are capable of attaining by our own good works. John represents the highest that any one can achieve; but the righteousness of Jesus is vastly superior.

Look at people who are under the law, such as Roman Catholic little old ladies crawling up the stairs of the 'scala sancta' on their arthritic knees, with their prayers and their beads, in the hope that they will escape from going to purgatory. Jesus came to set people free from that kind of guilt and oppression.

Seventy percent of people in Utah are Mormons. Utah has by far the highest suicide rate in America. Why? They are under the law. The guilt that comes from their inability to live up to the standard. Jesus came to set people free from that. Many Orthodox Jews are neurotic. Religion makes people nuts. Make no mistake, religion is a form of mental illness. How can sinful man possibly measure up the standards of a perfect and holy God? That is why God had to become a man to do something for us that we could never do.

Religion defeats the whole purpose of the gospel. Religion is the fundamental opposite of Christianity. People who are into religion are under the curse of the law. It does not matter if they are Jew or Gentile, but we are going to focus on Jews.

For as many as are of the works of the law are under a curse; for it is written, "Cursed is everyone who does not abide by all things written in the book of the law, to perform them."

Now that no one is justified by the Law before God is evident, for, "the righteous man shall live by faith." (Galatians 3:10-12).

"Cursed is everyone who does not abide by all things written in the book of the Law." This has a specific meaning for the Jews, but it applies to all fallen mankind. Just look at the terrible curses of Leviticus 26 or Deuteronomy 28.

I permitted Myself to be sought by those who did not ask for Me [the Gentiles]; *I permitted myself to be found by those who did not seek Me. I said, "Here am I, Here am I," to a nation* [the Gentiles] *which did not call on My name. I spread out My hands all day long to a rebellious people* [the Jews], *who walk in the way which is not good following their own thoughts…* (Isaiah 65:1-2).

Therefore, thus says the Lord God, behold My servants shall eat, but you [the Jews] *shall be hungry.*

Behold, My servants shall drink, but you shall be thirsty.

Behold, My servants shall rejoice, but you shall be put to shame.

Behold, My servants shall shout joyfully with a glad heart, but you shall cry out with a heavy heart, and you shall wail with a broken spirit.

And you will leave your name for a curse to My chosen ones, and the Lord God will slay you. But my servants will be called by another name [Christians] (Isaiah 65:13-15).

God has an end times purpose for Israel and the Jews, but they are under the curse. Unsaved Jewish people are accursed; they are under the curse of the law. All of fallen mankind is under the curse of the law, but especially the Jews because they had it in print.

Let me explain what the law means. The law is like a balloon, as Watchman Nee described it. Without helium in it, the law of gravity is always going to make the balloon fall to the ground. If you pump helium, which is lighter than air, into the balloon, the law of buoyancy is stronger than the law of gravity and the balloon will float. Helium is like the Holy Spirit. Only if you come under the law of grace and have God's Spirit dwelling in you, producing the righteousness of Jesus, can you lead a life pleasing to God. You are never going to keep that balloon floating with air. It takes something better than air; it takes a law stronger than gravity. That stronger law is grace. It is the New Covenant, which is stronger than the Old Covenant.

All of mankind is under the curse of the Old Covenant. The Jews had the law in print and, consequently, are more accountable. Judgment comes to the Jews first.

The gospel… is the power of God for salvation to everyone who believes, to the Jew first and also to the Gentile. There will be tribulation and distress for every soul of man who does evil, of the Jew first and also of the Gentile, but glory and honour and peace to every man who does good, to the Jew first and also to the Gentile (Romans 1:16; 2:9-10).

Because salvation is available to them first, the consequence of rejecting the gospel comes upon them first—the holocaust, the Spanish Inquisition, the crusades, the terrible sufferings of the Jewish people.

What did God say? "I will give you into the hands of your enemies." This is in no way to justify anti-semitism or the persecution of the Jews; it is to say that they will only be safe in the will of God. Once they go outside of it they have cursed themselves, because of the curse of the law.

Unsaved Jews—non Messianic Jews, Jewish people who do not follow Jesus as the Messiah—are accursed. Not only that, they are doubly accursed, because under the law there was a provision for sin.

With the sacrifices brought to the temple, offered by the proper priesthood, under the proper circumstances, if accompanied by faith and repentance, they had a sacrificial atonement.

The blood of these animals would cover the sin until Messiah came and took it away. But now there is no provision for them. There is no temple, and there is no high priesthood. The only temple now is the Body of Christ. In seven places the New Testament says that the church is the tabernacle.

My family and I celebrate Passover with lamb. Unsaved Jews eat the Passover with poultry. They testify to the fact that they have no lamb because they have no temple and no priesthood. Jewish believers have a temple and a priest. The new high priest is Jesus. We have a high priest, so we can partake of Passover with lamb. On the roof of every orthodox synagogue, you have the Hebrew term *Ichabod,* "the glory has departed," in recognition of the fact that, the temple was destroyed.

The religion of the Jews today is not the religion of Moses. Much the same as Roman Catholicism, Liberal Protestantism, Greek Orthodoxy, Mormonism and Jehovah Witnesses are not the Christianity of the New Testament, so Rabbinic Judaism is in no sense the Judaism of the Old Testament. It is a different religion begun by Rabbi Yochanan Ben Zacchai. They will not admit it, but their liturgy and festivals prove it. If it were the same thing, how come they do not eat the Passover as the Torah decrees? The Jews are accursed. Only Jesus could break that curse and He did break it. In three places the book of Hebrews tells us that Jesus died once and for all.

For it is fitting that we should have such a high priest, holy, innocent, undefiled, separated from sinners and exalted above the heavens; who does not need daily, like those high priests, to offer up sacrifices, first for his own sins, and then for the sins of the people, because this He did ONCE FOR ALL when He offered up Himself

(Hebrews 7:26-27).

But when Christ appeared as a high priest of the good things to come, He entered through the greater and more perfect tabernacle, not made with hands, that is to say, not of this creation; and not through the blood of goats and calves, but through His own blood, He entered the Holy Place ONCE FOR ALL, having obtained eternal redemption (Hebrews 9:11-12).

By this will we have been sanctified through the offering of the body of Jesus Christ ONCE FOR ALL (Hebrews 10:10).

Jesus became that curse and broke it. Every false version of Christianity denies the cross of Jesus in some way. Roman Catholicism, Jehovah Witnesses, Mormons, Copeland and Hagin—teaching that Jesus died, spiritually and became a satanic being—all of these things deny the cross. But Jesus was the perfect sacrifice, once and for all. He has broken forever the curse of the law from the lives of His people.

All things are new to those who are in Christ Jesus. But when you begin to say that something is not new, it becomes a subtle way of denying the sufficiency of Jesus' work on the cross.

When Jesus called Lazarus out of the tomb, He told the apostles, "You roll away the stone." Then Jesus commanded Lazarus to come out of the tomb. When Lazarus came forth, Jesus said to the apostles, "You unbind him." This is a midrashic picture of evangelism. The tomb is this fallen world. Rolling away the stone occurs when we witness to someone. The only thing we are doing is making it possible for them to hear the voice of Jesus. Only the Son of Man can call that which is dead unto life.

Some people say that if he did not say "Lazarus, come forth", every dead person in the world would have gotten up.

Rolling away the stone is evangelism. People can only come out of the tomb if they hear the voice of Jesus. Unless the Holy Spirit convicts them, unless the Father draws them and they hear Jesus' voice, they will not get saved. When they come out, Jesus says to us, "You unbind them." I do not deny the need for prayer, counselling, and discipleship. I do not deny all the other ways that Christians can be cursed that we have listed above. But Christians cannot be under the curse of the law unless they put themselves back under it by wilfully backsliding.

I used to go to a witch and she read my tarot cards. I could meet someone I did not know and tell them their zodiac sign and I was usually right. But the person who did those things is dead. The Jacob Prasch who was involved in witchcraft is dead.

The devil will always try to get you to deny the cross. He wants to get people caught up in saying things like: "Because my grandfather was a warlock, or because my granny was a witch, or whatever... therefore I am under a curse and everything is going wrong in my life."

The devil is a liar. Jesus said, "It is finished." When Jesus was crucified, I died with Him and so did you.

Now it is true that we die daily. Take up your cross and follow Him. The old creation is always there; we are living in the same old house. But spiritually we are new creations; that person is dead.

The devil will always try to get us to live in the old creation, and pretend we are not a new creation. He will always try to get us to live in the flesh.

When you begin saying, "Because of this and that and the other, I am cursed," you are putting yourself back under the law.

You are not cursed. You are a new creation in Christ Jesus. That curse was broken at the cross. Do not allow the devil to lie to you and tell you otherwise. Unbinding? Yes. Prayer? Yes. Counselling? Yes. Discipleship? Of course. But this "breaking of curses" process taught in so many churches today is simply a way of rejecting the work of the cross and placing yourself back under the curse of the law.

If there is some unconfessed sin in your life, repent of the sin. That is the solution. But forget about this "breaking the curse" nonsense.

If you are being persecuted for your faith and people are calling down evil upon you, yes, you are accursed. We are all cursed in that sense. Jesus will see us through it and—in His way and in His time—out of it.

But to say that the Old Testament curses are on you is a denial of the cross. You are a new creation. You may be bound; there may be things oppressing you psychologically and emotionally. You may need prayer and counselling, I do not deny that. I do not deny the idea of the strongholds of Satan in our lives, which are actually weaknesses in our old nature which the devil can exploit. They are not strongholds so much as they are weaknesses.

The more we live in the new creation, the more we will overcome the flesh. But people look for an instant solution. In other words, the flesh does not want to take up its cross and follow Jesus. We live in an 'instamatic' society. Instead of people taking up their cross and asking Jesus for the grace and persevering in faith and in prayer to live a holy life, they just want to go and get the demons cast out. Instead of focusing on your problems, say, "Lord, why do I have these problems? What are you trying to teach me? How are you trying to use this thing to make me more like Jesus? How are you going to use these problems to bring good into my life? How are you going to bless me through this suffering?" When God lets a bad thing happen to us, it is only to do good to us in the end. It is usually only in retrospect that you understand what He was doing. We walk by faith, not by sight (unless, of course, you follow Kenneth Hagin).

It is perfectly valid to recontextualise the gospel for our world view. Paul said, *I have became all things to all men, that I may by all means save some* (1 Corinthians 9:22).

My family and I do not eat pork or shellfish because it would be bad for my testimony to Jewish people. It is better for us not to do it, so we do not. All things are lawful, but not all things are helpful. It would not be right for me, but for you, go ahead; what do I care?

In this country, I am perfectly happy to take the Lord's Supper with either wine or with grape juice. I will do whatever your church does; it does not matter. But when I go to Ireland, where alcoholism is such a problem, I do not want to be seen touching alcohol in any kind of public format. Not because I have a problem taking the Lord's Supper with wine, but in that context it is not good for my testimony.

In our instamatic society people re-interpret the gospel in light of instant gratification. Recontextualization is right, but reinterpretation and redefinition is wrong. We live in a world of consumerism. Everything is consumption-oriented. The advertising industry is constantly urging people to consume. Prosperity theology is the gospel being redefined and reinterpreted in light of western consumerism.

We live in a high-tech society. "Get the right software for your hardware and your computer will do what you want it to do." So people think that the only thing we have to do is get the right church growth program and our church will grow. I am not against people being saved. I am saying that "getting the right program" will not bring revival.

We want things instantly. Taking up your cross and following Jesus is not easy. I do not care how many times you get the curses broken, that is not going to solve your problems. Any curse you were under was broken at the cross. It has nothing to do with what you did or your grandfather did before you were saved. All things are new to those who are in Christ Jesus. The devil wants you to deny that truth and deny the cross.

Now we die daily, that is true. It is through being identified with Jesus and his death and resurrection that we obtain freedom. It is not by getting curses broken. Live a crucified, resurrected life in the power of the Spirit and you will find freedom. Maybe the crucified life for you requires struggling in relationships or in finance or in health. Maybe that is your cross. All things will work together for good. God will set you free in His way and in His time, using the method He knows is best for you. The cross is a curse, but it is a necessary evil. Without it there is no resurrection. Through the cross, Jesus sets you free.

We can be taken lightly instead of being respected; we can be cursed in that way. Evil can be called down upon our nation. People can say bad things about us and curse us in anger. But the only way we can be placed back under the curse of the law is if we backslide into it. The only way a Christian can be cursed in that way is by putting himself under it, by rejecting Jesus.

All things are new to those who are in Christ Jesus. His cross is sufficient once and for all. The only time you are going to be cursed is when you throw the cross away!

Do you want to be a Christian under a curse? Throw the cross away. Do you want to be a Christian free from the curse? Take up your cross and follow Jesus.

HOUSE OF DAVID: HOUSE OF SAUL

*H*EAR *the word of the Lord, you who tremble at His word: Your brothers who hate you, who exclude you for My name's sake, have said, 'Let the Lord be glorified, that we may see your joy' But they will be put to shame* (Isaiah 66:5). When your brethren hate you and exclude you for the sake of the Lord's name your life becomes difficult.

The book of Judges is a book about wars. It is Jews fighting Amalekites, Canaanites, Philistines. It gives all the statistics of how many were killed, how many were captured. The worst of those wars was the last war in Judges. And the worst war, the bloodiest war with the most fatalities, was not against Amalekites, Canaanites or Philistines, it involved Jews fighting other Jews.

What caused Paul the most consternation? Was it being dragged before the Roman authorities, flogged in the synagogue, attacked by mobs in Ephesus? Read his epistles; these things did not cause him the most grief. Persecution is not what distressed him. Rather, it was false brethren, false teachers and false prophets trying to seduce the churches that he planted.

I am not afraid of going against Freemasonry, or Rome, or Orthodox Rabbis, or Islam, or New Age, or the homosexuals. Those are not what I fear. The kind of war I dread is when you have to pick up your sword and go against your brethren.

In the last war in Judges they had no choice. A woman's body was hacked into fragments, and divided. And the Body of Christ in the western world is being hacked to death and divided. We have no choice but to pick up the sword, the body is being hacked to death.

Look at some of the doctrines that are being taught today. E.W.Kenyon was the patriarch of all of it. "Jesus died spiritually." He says that Jesus did not win the victory on the cross.

On the cross Jesus said, "It is finished," but, according to Kenyon, that was not the victory. Jesus died and rose again, but Kenyon says that Jesus descended into hell and became of one nature with Satan. Jesus was born again in hell—that is the 'gospel' of Kenneth Copeland and Kenneth Hagin. They believe that the Lord Jesus Christ died on the cross, but the victory over sin and death was not accomplished on the cross.

The Body is being hacked to death. "You don't have to suffer, God wants you rich." By virtue of the fact that you live in a western democracy, you *are* rich. You are better off than at least two thirds of the people in the world. The body is being hacked to death by a gospel of mammon which these false teachers are calling the "gospel of Jesus" and "faith prosperity."

But those who want to get rich fall into temptation and a snare and many foolish and harmful desires which plunge men into ruin and destruction. For the love of money is a root of all sorts of evil, and some by longing for it have wandered away from the faith... (1 Timothy 6:9-10).

Hebrews 11, the 'faith chapter,' talks more about faith than all the rest of the New Testament put together. It does not mention money once, only alluding to wealth to tell you about those who could have had it, but turned their backs on it for the sake of the kingdom (Hebrews 11:26).

The body is being hacked to death. It is very difficult when you have to lift your sword against your brother.

Now there was a long war between the house of Saul and the house of David; and David grew steadily stronger, but the House of Saul grew weaker continually (2 Samuel 3:1).

David and Saul both had a common enemy, the Canaanites and Philistines who were over-running the land. The enemy prevailed because the leadership of Israel had become so corrupt. David could do nothing about it until the leadership was replaced. He could not replace the leadership because Saul was God's anointed. He was stuck in a situation where wickedness was prevailing, where God's people were being defeated.

And that is exactly what is going on today. God's people are being defeated and there is going to be a long war between the house of David and the house of Saul. But the house of David will get stronger and stronger, and the house of Saul will get weaker and weaker. The only question is, which house are you going to belong to?

If you want to, you can have your ears tickled with blab-it-and-grab-it, western consumerism, which is all the 'prosperity gospel' is; people trying to redefine the truth of the bible in light of western consumerism. The people who subscribe to these errors do so because they want to believe lies.

They did not receive the love of the truth so as to be saved. And for this reason God will send upon them a deluding influence so that they might believe what is false (2 Thessalonians 2:10-11).

But there is something much more difficult and much more painful than that here. We all know the story of King David and how Saul hated him and tried to kill him. The one sticking point was Jonathan. Jonathan loved David. Jonathan knew that Saul had become corrupt and lost God's calling and blessing. Jonathan knew his father was no good. He knew the house of Saul was under the curse of God. He knew David was right. He knew David was an innocent victim who was being persecuted. He knew David was God's chosen. He knew it all, but Jonathan was too cemented to the house of Saul to make the break. David is always a type of Jesus. Jesus said, *"He who loves father or mother more than Me, is not worthy of Me"* (Matthew 10:37). That alludes to the situation of Jonathan.

Are you part of the house of David or the house of Saul? To be part of the house of Saul does not require you to believe false doctrine yourself. It just means that you are committed to established structures, churches and denominations that have gone into this error. Is your denomination more important to you than what God is saying?

Then Samuel took the flask of oil, and poured it on his head, kissed him and said, "Has not the Lord anointed you a ruler over His inheritance?" (1 Samuel 10:1).

Remember different liquids represent the Holy Spirit in different aspects. In this case it is oil, which speaks of the anointing. The Holy Spirit really was poured out on the house of Saul. It was authentic, but if something ends in the flesh, it does not matter if it began in the Spirit or if it was always in error to begin with. If something is wrong now, it does not matter if it began good or if it began bad.

I do not doubt for one second that thirty years ago there was a genuine outpouring of God's Spirit. I know that was true, but I am just as convinced that it went into the flesh a long time ago. Every single charismatic movement in the history of the church has ended the same way. The Montanists - experiential theology, Muenster Anabaptists and early Pentecostals—crazy doctrines, Quakers—inner light. It is always the Spirit and the Truth. But they said, "Give us the Spirit, we don't want the Truth." The word of God tells us what is flesh and what is Spirit.

As you did not obey the Lord and did not execute His fierce wrath upon Amalek, so the Lord has done this thing to you this day. Moreover the Lord will also deliver Israel along with you into the hand of the Philistines, therefore tomorrow you and your sons will be with me. Indeed the Lord will give over the army of Israel into the hands of the Philistines (1 Samuel 28:18).

Saul started out with the anointing, but God rejected him.

Then Samuel said to Saul "The Lord sent me to anoint you as king over His people, over Israel; now therefore, listen to the words of the Lord.

"Thus says the Lord of hosts, I will punish Amalek for what he did to Israel, how he set himself against him on the way while he was coming up from Egypt. Now go and strike Amalek and utterly destroy all that he has, and do not spare him; but put to death both man and woman, child and infant, ox and sheep, camel and donkey" (1 Samuel 15:1-3).

But Saul did not do it.

But Saul and the people spared Agag and the best of the sheep, the oxen, the fatlings, the lambs, and all that was good, and were not willing to destroy them utterly; but everything despised and worthless, that they utterly destroyed. Then the word of the Lord came to Samuel, saying, "I regret that I have made Saul king, for he has turned back from following Me, and has not carried out My commands. And Samuel was distressed and cried out to the Lord all night (1 Samuel 15:9-11).

Amalek, also known as Agag, was an ancient enemy. The enmity goes back to the time of Moses; it resurfaces in the person of Haman, a descendant of Agag, in the book of Esther. This enmity had persisted over hundreds of years, back to the Babylonian captivity. The old enemy remains the enemy. It does not change. Saul was told what Moses was told, what Joshua was told: These are your ancient enemies, get rid of them.

Who are our ancient enemies? We are told in the New Testament that we struggle not against flesh and blood. As Christians, we love our enemies. There is a big difference between loving people in false religions, and loving the false religions. We are to hate idolatry, sin, and superstition. I hate it because it is leading people to hell by the tens of millions.

Saul tried to keep the parts he thought were acceptable. Saul tried to make peace with the ancient enemy.

When you try to make peace with your ancient enemy, the ancient enemy comes back and devours you, just like it did in the book of Esther.

You can look back and see in history that more bible believing Christians were killed by papal Rome than were killed by pagan Rome.

John Bunyan called it a "Two Headed Giant"—one called Pagan, and the other called Pope! You may say, "They did that five hundred years ago, they did that sixteen hundred years ago, but they would not do that in the 20th century!" Hitler, Himmler and Goebbels were all Catholics, and most of Hitler's deputies were Jesuit educated.

Franz von Papen, vice-chancellor to Hitler and a privy chamberlain to Pope Pius 12th, said, "The Third Reich was the first power in the world, not only to recognize, but also to put into practice the high principles of the Roman Catholic papacy."

Joachim von Ribbentropp, Hitler's advisor in foreign affairs and papal envoy, said, "Adolph Hitler is the envoy of God."

Some believe that they would not do that in the 20th century. Saul thought that Agag would not do what they did in the days of Moses. Esther did not think that Haman would have done it either. The Roman Catholic church condemns those who say the church must not use violent force. There are pictures of nuns marching with gestapo officers to get Jewish children and take them out to be killed. The simple basic constitutional principle of Roman Catholicism is always the same. Rome has not changed; Agag has not changed.

The first mistake of the charismatic movement was experiential theology. The second was failing to drive out the enemies of God. When the charismatic renewal happened in the Roman Church, the Holy Spirit was calling God's people to come out of false religion.

"Ho there! Flee from the land of the north," declares the Lord, *"For I have dispersed you as the four winds of the heavens."* declares the Lord, *"Ho Zion! Escape, you who are living with the daughter of Babylon"* (Zech. 2:6-7).

And I heard another voice from heaven, saying, 'Come out of her, My people, that you may not participate in her sins and that you may not receive of her plagues; for her sins have piled up as high as heaven, and God has remembered her iniquities' (Revelation 18:4-5).

It does not say they are not God's people. But to be His people and stay in a church that says you are going to burn in purgatory for your own sins, when the bible says that the blood of Jesus cleanses us from all sins, is sin. The Hebrew word for 'to worship' is the same word as 'prostrate, genuflect.' It is the same exact word. Praying to the dead and genuflecting before statues (practising idolatry) is sin. Praying to the dead is contacting a familiar spirit. It is a sin. You cannot practice Roman Catholicism without sinning. Praying to the dead is sin. Idolatry—Mary worship, kissing statues—is sin. The Roman Catholic church has a history of murdering true Christians and, if they get their chance, they will do it again. Babylon cannot be healed.

Saul's second mistake was his failure to go to the Word of God. The Torah showed clearly how to get rid of Amalek.

But Saul invented his own doctrine and his own code of practice. As a result, he lost his anointing and calling. The charismatic movement has done the same thing. They did not go to the Word of God, but invented their own doctrine and code of practice.

Thirty years ago the charismatic movement happened in the United States, and other places around the world. The charismatic renewal was supposed to bring spiritual and moral restoration to the British Isles, and bring reconciliation between Catholics and Protestants. They were going to win the country back for Jesus. The charismatic renewal was going to bring spiritual and moral restoration to the USA. Is there less crime, less divorce, less homosexuality, less substance abuse, less racism now? No, there is more of all of it!

The charismatic movement has not been able to renew the church, let alone the country. It has not moved the church to repentance, let alone the nation. Thirty years ago you would not have found Anglican bishops denying the virgin birth or the resurrection of Jesus Christ, nor Hindu gods being worshipped in Anglican churches, nor professed homosexuals in a Methodist pulpit. Not only is society worse off than it was before the charismatic renewal, but the church is worse off.

Every Christian is a priest. We are all supposed to bring a sacrifice of praise, and lay our life down, not loving our life in this world. *"If anyone wishes to come after Me, let him deny himself and take up his cross daily and follow Me"* (Luke 9:23). I have dropped my cross many times. I thank God for Jesus, who helps me pick it up again and keep following him. My old nature and my flesh do not want to.

So far, seven bishops and hundreds of clergy have either walked out, or are planning to walk out, of the Church of England over the ordination of women priests. When the virgin birth was denied, no one walked out. When the resurrection of Jesus Christ was denied, no one walked out. When bishops began laying hands on homosexuals and consecrating them for the ministry, no one walked out. When Hindu gods were worshipped in Anglican churches, no one walked out. Now homosexual and lesbian Anglican clergy met on national TV at Southwark Cathedral, but no one left after that either.

These people do not care about God's Word or God's Truth. They do not care about God's Son. They only care about their religion. The house of Saul is always bent on one thing: self-preservation.

And he captured Agag the king of the Amalekites alive, and utterly destroyed all the people with the edge of the sword. But Saul and the people spared Agag and the best of the sheep, the oxen, the fatlings, the lambs, and all that was good, and were not willing to destroy them utterly; but everything despised and worthless, that they utterly destroyed.

Then the word of the Lord came to Samuel, saying, "I regret that I have made Saul king, for he has turned back from following Me, and has not carried out My commands."

And Samuel was distressed and cried out to the Lord all night. And Samuel rose early in the morning to meet Saul, and it was told Samuel saying, "Saul came to Carmel, and behold, he set up a monument for himself, then turned and proceeded on down to Gilgal" (1 Samuel 15:8-12).

Saul set up a monument for himself. The Sauls of the modern church are also busily engaged in setting up monuments for themselves.

And Samuel came to Saul, and Saul said to him, "Blessed are you of the Lord! I have carried out the command of the Lord." But Samuel said, "What then is this bleating of the sheep in my ears, and the lowing of the oxen which I hear?" (1 Samuel 15:13-14).

The house of Saul thinks it is in God's grace, thinks it is in God's favour, thinks it is in God's blessing, until the real prophetic voice comes and tells them the truth.

And Saul said, "They have brought them from the Amalekites, for the people spared the best of the sheep and oxen, to sacrifice unto the Lord your God; but the rest we have utterly destroyed" (1 Samuel 15:15).

"There are good things in the Roman Catholic church that we can draw from," say some people. But if you knew something was part rotten, would you eat it?

Then Samuel said to Saul, "Wait and let me tell you what the Lord said to me last night." And he said to him, "Speak!"

And Samuel said, "Is it not true, though you were little in your own eyes, you were made the head of the tribes of Israel? And the Lord anointed thee king over Israel?" (1 Samuel 15:16-17).

The people asked for a king. They always want a flesh leader instead of looking to God. "Give us a leader, or give us a king." When people ask for a leader or king, there is always something wrong with their relationship with Jesus. People refuse to understand that they can only follow a human leader as far as that person has a relationship with God, not one bit further. If that leader has no relationship with God, then you will be in the same confusion and doubt as the leader. What did Paul say? *Be imitators of me, just as I also am of Christ* (1 Corinthians 11:1).

Follow me to the exact extent that I am following Jesus. Agree with me to the exact extent that what I say agrees with the Word of God. Trust me to the exact extent that I am trusting God. No more. We have a king; we should not try to make other people into our king. *The Lord sent you on a mission, and said, 'Go and utterly destroy the sinners, the Amalekites, and fight against them until they are exterminated.*

"Why then did you not obey the voice of the Lord, but rushed upon the spoil and did what was evil in the sight of the Lord?" (1 Samuel 15:18-19).

We are showing our treasures to the king of Babylon. When you send converts back to the Roman Catholic church, as Billy Graham is doing, you are showing your treasures to the king of Babylon (2 Kings 20:12-18). When you do this, it is only a matter of time before the king of Babylon will come and take the treasure.

And Saul said to Samuel, "I did obey the voice of the Lord, and went on the mission on which the Lord sent me..." (1 Samuel 15:20).

They always defend their actions. They insist they are obeying the Lord, they insist they are following him. But the Word of God says differently. They say, "Do not talk to us about doctrine; doctrine divides." The New Testament contains twice as much exhortation to right doctrine as it does right conduct. Why? If we do not know right doctrine, we will not know right conduct. The purpose of doctrine is to divide!

"But the people took some of the spoil, sheep and oxen, the choicest of the things devoted to destruction, to sacrifice to the Lord your God at Gilgal" (1 Samuel 15:21).

The bad leaders always blame the people. "The people took the spoil. We cannot control the people." Those in leadership were given a job to do and they are responsible. They are supposed to be God's authority in that relationship.

And Samuel said, "Has the Lord as much delight in burnt offerings and sacrifices as in obedience to the voice of the Lord? Behold, to obey is better than sacrifice, and to heed than the fat of rams. For rebellion is as the sin of divination, and insubordination is as iniquity and idolatry. Because you have rejected the word of the Lord, He has also rejected you from being king." (1 Samuel 15:22-23).

They will bring a sacrifice of praise, but they will not obey the bible.

Then Saul said to Samuel, "I have sinned; I have indeed transgressed the command of the Lord and your words, because I feared the people and listened to their voice. Now therefore, please pardon my sin and return with me, that I may worship the Lord." But Samuel said to Saul, "I will not return with you; for you have rejected the word of the Lord, and the Lord has rejected you from being king over Israel" (1 Samuel 15:24-26).

Once people have openly rejected the teaching of the word of the Lord, you can go no further with them. You have no basis of fellowship. *Can two walk together, except they be agreed?* (Amos 3:3). We are talking about basics—salvation, the authority of scripture, the person of Christ.

The bible says if people predict things that do not happen, get away from them. When people prefer the teachings of Toronto/Brownsville, despite knowing the contradiction between what the bible says and what their leaders do, we should get away from them. People who will not listen to truth are in rebellion, and rebellion is as witchcraft. These movements openly defy the clear word of God.

There have been a number of predictions made by people like John Wimber, Paul Cain and Gerald Coates, predictions that did not happen.

Their false predictions were published in newspapers and on secular television, resulting in brutal mocking of Christians when they failed to happen.

When Gerald Coates was challenged over his false prophecy, he refused to take any responsibility for his actions. Both Rick Joyner and John Kilpatrick have made major predictions that failed to happen and people still follow them. This is rebellion, the same sin as witchcraft.

The people who follow Coates, Joyner and Kilpatrick cannot dispute that their leaders have predicted things that did not come to pass. They cannot dispute that the word of God says we should not follow them. But they do not want to obey the word of God. They prefer rebellion, witchcraft.

Once they reject the word of the Lord, there is no basis for truth, no fellowship to be had with them. Bible teaching in the charismatic movement has been so shallow that most of these people are doing it out of ignorance rather than wilful rebellion. But it is different with the leaders. They should all be called to repentance. They should not be allowed any form of ministry. They have deceived and mislead so many people.

So Samuel said to him, "The Lord has torn the kingdom of Israel from you today and has given it to your neighbour who is better than you. And also the Glory of Israel will not lie or change His mind; for He is not a man that He should change His mind" (1 Samuel 15:28).

And He has still not changed his mind. When the house of Saul goes wrong, God begins to build the house of David.

God began teaching David from the time he was a little boy. God trains people for the extraordinary in the ordinary.

How was David able to kill Goliath? When he was a shepherd boy, he went around with his slingshot killing wolves that attacked the sheep.

A faithful shepherd [same word in Hebrew as 'pastor'], will be given more responsibility by God.

For some of these men today, the sheep merely represent stepping stones for advancement on the speaking circuit.

The first lesson David learned was not to wear Saul's armour. Those who will be in the house of David have to learn the same lesson. You cannot wear Saul's armour, it is too cumbersome.

Now it came about in those days that the Philistines gathered their armed camps for war to fight against Israel. And Achish said to David, "Know assuredly that you will go out with me in the camp, you and your men." And David said to Achish, "Very well, you shall know what your servant can do." So Achish said to David, "Very well, I will make you my bodyguard for life."

Now Samuel was dead, and all Israel had lamented him and buried him in Ramah his own city. And Saul had removed from the land those who were mediums and spiritists. So the Philistines gathered together and came and camped in Shunem; and Saul gathered all Israel together and they camped in Gilboa.

When Saul saw the camp of the Philistines, he was afraid and his heart trembled greatly. When Saul inquired of the Lord, the Lord did not answer him, either by dreams or by Urim nor by prophets. Then Saul said to his servants, "Seek for me a woman who is a medium, that I may go to her and inquire of her." And his servants said, "Behold, there is a woman who is a medium at Endor" (1 Samuel 28:1-7).

Saul stopped hearing from the Lord. Today the charismatic leaders are really afraid. Why were Wimber, Paul Gain and Gerald Coates wrong? They talk big, but they are afraid. They know their own track record. They know they have been around thirty years and, things have gone from bad to worse, and from worse to worse yet.

That is why they need one gimmick after another, like the 'laughing revival,' to keep people unknowing as to what is really going on. These people stopped hearing from the Lord a long time ago. Benny Hinn said that he goes to the Forest Lawn Cemetery in Los Angeles, California, to commune with the dead. He gets his 'anointing' off the dead bodies of

Aimee McPherson and Kathryn Kuhlman. When you do not hear from the Lord, you go to witches. That is what happened then, and that is what is happening today.

But the house of David grows stronger and stronger. How does it begin? 'Davids' are shepherd boys. *He who is faithful in a very little thing, is faithful also in much* (Luke 16:10). Christians who are already faithfully taking care of those God has already given them—good husbands, good fathers, good pastors, good house group leaders—are the kinds of people God is going to use to take care of the whole flock. God trains people for the extraordinary in the ordinary. The last thing Goliath would have expected was a teenage boy who was a dead aim with a slingshot—the one thing that could have stopped him. The kinds of people God is going to raise up will be people that Islam, New Age, Rome, homosexuals and Freemasons will never expect. These are going to be people God has been training for a long time; dead shots with a sling. And then God will begin to build his house.

One gets stronger while one gets weaker. He takes his calling from the house of Saul, but it runs on inertia. It has lost the anointing, but God leaves it to run on for a time until the house of David is built. When you see the present spiritual seduction taking place, you can be sure of three things:

1. God will raise up prophetic voices against it. They might not be listened to, but they will be heard, the same as with Samuel.

2. There will be a faithful remnant. The remnant will hear, they will listen and respond.

3. God will build a new house.

And everyone who was in distress, and everyone who was in debt, and everyone who was discontented, gathered to him; and he became captain over them. Now there were about four hundred men with him (1 Samuel 22:2).

The outcasts of Israel gathered to David. I do not expect the pastors of the bigger churches or the members of executives to join the house of David. Very few of them will join. At best, they will be Jonathans. It will be people like us—losers, outcasts, nobodies, the unfashionable. We are nothings now, but what were we before? We have nothing that is not the result of Jesus having saved us.

These are the names of the mighty men whom David had: Joshebbasshebeth a

Tahchemonite, chief of the captains, he was called Adino the Eznite; because of eight hundred slain by him at one time; and after him was Eleazar the son of Dodo the Ahohite, one of the three mighty men with David when they defied the Philistines who were gathered there to battle and the men of Israel had withdrawn. He arose and struck the Philistines until his hand was weary and clung to the sword, and the Lord bought about a great victory that day, and the people returned after him only to strip the slain. Now after him was Shammah, the son of Agee the Hararite. And the Philistines were gathered into a troop, where there was a plot of ground full of lentils, and the people fled from the Philistines.

But he took his stand in the midst of the plot, defended it and struck the Philistines, and the Lord brought about a great victory (1 Samuel 23:8–12).

So the three mighty men broke through the camp of the Philistines, and drew water from the well of Beth-Lehem which is by the gate, and took it and brought it to David (1 Samuel 23:16).

The so-called mighty men of Israel today, the great Christian leaders, run away from homosexuals, run away from New Age, run away from Roman Catholicism; they run away from everything. They do not have the necessary courage to fight.

God is going to raise up little boys with slingshots. God is going to gather the mighty men.

But who are these mighty men of David; who are these commanders? They are the same ones mentioned in 1 Samuel 22:2—those who were in distress, who were in debt, who were discontent, the nothings and the nobodies. God takes the losers and makes them winners. He takes the nobodies and makes them commanders. Where did He do it? Where did He teach them how to become the great men? Where did they learn how to become generals?

Now David became aware that Saul had come out to seek his life when David was in the wilderness of Ziph, at Horesh (1 Samuel 23:15).

There are two kinds of trials in the bible: the valley and the wilderness. The valley is a short trial, but the wilderness is a long series of trials, like the Jews wandering in the wilderness for forty years. The wilderness, by nature, is a place of death. That is why the second generation entered the holy land. The first generation died in the wilderness. Only the new creation could go to heaven and to the promised land, not the old one. God uses the wilderness to destroy the flesh, to burn off the old creation.

It was a long war, David became stronger, Saul became weaker. But God did not remove the house of Saul altogether, until David was ready. Those who are to be made into the mighty ones of Israel, whom God will use to rebuild the Body of Christ in this country, are already going through a long sojourn in the wilderness.

"And the Lord will repay each man for his righteousness and his faithfulness; for the Lord delivered you into my hand today but I refused to stretch out my hand against the Lord's anointed" (1 Samuel 26:23).

"So what that Benny Hinn communes with the dead? Don't touch God's anointed! So what that Oral Roberts said God would kill him if he didn't raise seven or eight million dollars? Don't touch God's anointed!"

David did not touch Saul because he was God's anointed, but did God ever stop Samuel or David from telling the truth about Saul? The verse is not even concerned with what they are talking about.

"Therefore let all the house of Israel know for certain that God has made Him [Jesus] both Lord and Christ - this Jesus whom you crucified" (Acts 2:36).

'Christ' in Greek is *ho christos,* in Hebrew is *Ha Mashiach,* and in both languages means literally 'the anointed one'. There is only ONE 'anointed one' in scripture and that is Jesus.

Behold, how good and how pleasant it is, for brothers to dwell together in unity! It is like the precious oil upon the head, coming down upon the beard, even Aaron's beard, coming down upon the edge of his robes (Psalm 133:1).

Aaron, the high priest, was an Old Testament type of Jesus. He was anointed—the oil was poured on his head, then it ran off onto his body.

For the husband is the head of the wife, as Christ also is the head of the church (Ephesians 5:23). We are the Body of Christ. To be 'anointed' we must be attached to the body and under the head. Jesus is the anointed one. We have no anointing, except under his headship, as members of the body. These people proclaiming themselves to be 'anointed' are not attached to the body and they are not under the headship of Christ.

Before Jesus was anointed for power, for dominion, for victory, Jesus was anointed for burial. Before anyone is anointed for ministry, they are first anointed for burial. Paul said the proof of his anointing was not that he did miracles, signs and wonders, or that he planted churches or that he wrote half the New Testament. *Rather, I bear on my body the brand marks of Jesus* (Galatians 6:17). *Always carrying about in the body the dying of Jesus, that the life of Jesus also may be manifested in our body* (2 Corinthians 4:10). Because he was anointed for burial, God could anoint Paul for power.

Then Samuel took the horn of oil and anointed him in the midst of his brothers; and the Spirit of the Lord came mightily upon David from that day forward. And Samuel arose and went to Ramah. Now the spirit of the Lord departed from Saul, and an evil spirit from the Lord terrorised him (1 Samuel 16:13-14).

At best, much of the hyper-charismatic phenomena you see today is soulish. Some of it is demonic, evil. Healings claimed to be by Mary are not from God, who will not give His glory to another. There is no doubt that Saul came under some demonic deception and I am sure it is working again today.

And David was prospering in all his ways for the Lord was with him. When Saul saw that he was prospering greatly, he dreaded him (1 Samuel 18:14-15). A time will come when the house of David will begin to emerge from the wilderness, and the house of Saul will become very envious. They are going to despise you, and hate you, and want to kill you. By that time you will be dealing with something openly satanic, an evil spirit tormenting. Remember, the house of Saul is only concerned with one thing, self preservation.

Then David inquired of the Lord, saying, "Shall I go up against the Philistines? Wilt Thou give them into my hand?" And the Lord said to David, "Go up, for I will certainly give the Philistines into your hand" (2 Samuel 5:19).

There will come a time when the house of David will do the things that charismatics and pentecostals cannot do. They cannot attack New Age, ecumenism, homosexuality, or Islam, they do not have the courage. They only care about preserving their positions, their little empires.

When the house of David is built, there will be people that know how to slay eight hundred. They will know how to go up against New Age, homosexuals, Rome, Islam, and the Lord will give them the victory.

Then all the tribes of Israel came to David at Hebron [place of fellowship] *and said, "Behold, we are your bone and your flesh".*

"Previously when Saul was king over us, you were the one who lead Israel out and in. And the Lord said to you, 'You will shepherd My people Israel, and you will be a ruler over Israel.'"

So all the elders of Israel came to the king at Hebron, and King David made a covenant with them before the Lord at Hebron; then they anointed David king over

Israel (2 Samuel 5:1-3).

There will come a time that these people will arrive as refugees to the new house. They will come to the place of fellowship because the house of Saul will have been destroyed. The ones that have remained faithful are going to join themselves to the new house when the time comes. With one unfortunate and tragic exception. This will be the most difficult thing to come to pass in the next few years. They are the Jonathans.

And the Philistines overtook Saul and his sons; and the Philistines killed Jonathan and Abinadab and Malchi-shua the sons of Saul (1 Samuel 31:2).

Then David took hold of his clothes and tore them, and so also did all the men who were with him. And they mourned and wept and fasted until evening for Saul and for his son Jonathon and for the people of the Lord and the house of Israel, because they had fallen by the sword (2 Samuel 1:11).

This will be the most difficult aspect—the Jonathans. Jonathan knew David was right. He knew David was commissioned by God, that he was innocent and righteous. Jonathan knew his father's house had gone wrong. He knew his father was corrupt. He knew the land was being over run, and they were losing everything because of his father's house. But Jonathan could not break with his father.

There are people out there today that know things are wrong, but they cannot leave. Those people who attach themselves to Saul, and cannot leave, will die on Mount Gilboa. That will be the most difficult thing to face. There are people whom you know and love, who are fed up with what is going on, who can see all this error for what it is. But they do not, have the courage of their convictions. Which house are you going to join? You will be of the house of Saul or the house of David.

You will have to come into the wilderness, where God is building it. You have to expect that the house of Saul is going to hate you and persecute you. You have to understand that you cannot wear Saul's armour. You will have to understand that these people are still our brethren, for better or worse.

Touch not God's anointed. You can tell the truth about them, but only God can remove them. We have to endure the pain and anguish that David experienced over Jonathan.

A time will come when the house of Saul will fall. How much longer can it keep going? It lurches from one gimmick to another, one trend to another, one line of hype to another. David's house will stand. It will stand at Hebron, the place of fellowship, and then others will join themselves to it. When that day comes, the Lord will give the victory over the Philistines, the Amalekites, the Canaanites, Islam, New Age, Freemasonry, Rome, and homosexual lobbying.

The house of David or the house of Saul? There is plenty of room in both. The choice is yours. If you want to join the house of David, now is your opportunity.

A PROPHET LIKE MOSES

*B*ut the prophet who shall speak a word presumptuously in my Name, which I have not commanded him to speak, or which he shall speak in the name of other gods, that prophet shall die (Deuteronomy 18:20).

It does not matter if a person predicts something in the name of the Lord because they are inspired by a demon, or if they do it by the futility of their own mind. Either way, a false prophet is a false prophet.

And you may say in your heart, "How shall we know the word which the Lord has not spoken?" When a prophet speaks in the name of the Lord, if the thing does not come about or come true, that is the thing which the Lord has not spoken. The prophet has spoken it presumptuously; you shall not be afraid of him (Deuteronomy 18:21-22).

Then Jeremiah the prophet said to Rananiah the prophet, "Listen now, Hananiah, the Lord has not sent you, and you have made this people trust in a lie.

Therefore thus says the Lord, 'Behold, I am about to remove you from the face of the earth'" (Jeremiah 28:15-16).

Hananiah predicted things that did not happen.

Then the Lord said to me, "The prophets are prophesying falsehood in my Name. I have neither sent them nor commanded them nor spoken to them; they are prophesying to you a false vision, divination, futility and the deception of their own minds" (Jeremiah 14:14).

These false prophets were deceived by what was in their own mind. There were a lot of false prophets running around in Jeremiah's day. But even after their prophesies were proven to be false, people continued to follow them.

The prophets prophesy falsely and the priests rule on their own authority; and My people love it so! But what will you do at the end of it? (Jeremiah 5:31)

It does not say they are not His people and it does not say they are not prophets. But He does say that they prophesy falsely and the people love it so.

When Jesus warned about false prophets in the last days, many people think He was talking about the Jehovah Witnesses, the Mormons, the Hare Krishnas, etc. There is no doubt in my mind that the proliferation of these cults is of some prophetic significance, and they are certainly false prophets. But those are not the false prophets Jesus was warning about. He said, "if possible the elect will be deceived."

The Talmud says that Deuteronomy 18:20 is about the Messiah. We know that it is about Jesus, who was a prophet like Moses.

Now a new king arose over Egypt, who did not know Joseph. And he said to his people, "Behold, the people of the sons of Israel are more and mightier than we. Come let us deal wisely with them, lest they multiply and in the event of war, they also join themselves to those who hate us, and fight against us, and depart from the land." So they appointed taskmasters over them to afflict them with hard labour. And they built for Pharaoh storage cities; Pithom and Raamses (Exodus 1:8-14). Moses was born under an oppressive, foreign rule.

Now it come about in those days that a decree went out from Caesar Augustus, that a census be taken of all the inhabited earth. This was the first census taken while Quirinius was governor of Syria (Luke 2:1). Jesus was born under an oppressive foreign rule.

Then the king of Egypt spoke to the Hebrew midwives, one of whom was named Shiphrah and the other was named Puah; and he said, "When you are helping the Hebrew women to give birth and see them upon the birthstool, if it is a son, then you shall put him to death; but if it is a daughter, then she shall live" (Exodus 1:15-16). A wicked king decreed that Moses and the male Jewish children be killed.

Then when Herod saw that he had been tricked by the magi, he became very enraged, and sent and slew all the male children who were in Bethlehem and all its environs, from two years old and under, according to the time which he had ascertained from the Magi (Matthew 2:16). A wicked king decreed that Jesus and the male Jewish children be killed.

And the woman conceived and bore a son; and when she saw that he was beautiful she hid him for three months (Exodus 2:2).

By faith Moses, when he was born, was hidden for three months by his parents, because they saw he was a beautiful child; and they were not afraid of the king's edict (Hebrews 11). Moses' life was saved and preserved through the faith of his parents.

Now when they had departed, behold, an angel of the Lord appeared to Joseph in a dream, saying, "Arise and take the child and His mother, and flee to Egypt, and remain there until I tell you for Herod is going to search for the child to destroy him" (Matthew 2:13-14). Jesus' life was saved and preserved through the faith of His parents.

And the child grew, and she brought him to Pharaoh's daughter, and he became her son. And she named him Moses, and said, "Because I drew him out of the water" (Exodus 2:10). Moses received protection in Egypt for a time.

And he arose and took the child and His mother by night, and departed for Egypt; and was there until the death of Herod, that what was spoken by the Lord through the prophet might be fulfilled, saying, "Out of Egypt did I call My Son" (Matthew 2:14-15). Jesus received protection in Egypt for a time.

Then Miriam and Aaron spoke against Moses... "Has the Lord indeed spoken only through Moses? Has he not spoken through us as well?" Now the man Moses was very humble, more than any man that was on the face of the earth (Numbers 12:3). There were other people trying to compete with Moses because of his wisdom.

And it came about that after three days they found him in the temple, sitting in the midst of the teachers, both listening to them, and asking them question. And all who heard Him were amazed at His understanding and answers (Luke 2:46-47).

Jesus, even from the earliest days of His youth, demonstrated tremendous wisdom and understanding, and others wanted to compete with Him, but they could not do it.

Now when the people saw that Moses delayed to come down from the mountain, the people assembled about Aaron, and said to him, "Come, make us a god who will go before us; as for this Moses, the man who brought us up from the land of Egypt, we do not know what has become of him" (Exodus 32:1).

Moses was rejected for a time by the people of Israel.

But the governor answered and said to them, "Which of the two do you want me to release for you?" And they said, "Barabbas." And Pilate said to them, "Then what shall I do with Jesus who is called the Messiah?" They all said, "Let Him be crucified" (Matthew 27-22).

Toward the end of His life, Jesus told the Jews, *"You shall not see Me until you say 'Blessed is he who comes in the name of the Lord'"* (Matthew 23:39). *For I do not want you, brethren, to be uninformed of this mystery lest you be wise in your own estimation, that a partial hardening has happened to Israel until the fullness of the Gentiles has come in* (Romans 11:25). Jesus was rejected for a time by the people of Israel.

And he [Moses] went out the next day and behold, two Hebrews were fighting with each other; and he said to the offender, "Why are you striking your companion?" But he said, "Who made you a prince or judge over us?" When Pharaoh heard of this matter, he tried to kill Moses. But Moses fled from the presence of Pharaoh and settled in the land of Midian. And Moses was willing to dwell with the man, and he gave his daughter Zipporah to Moses (Exodus 2:14,15,21). Moses was rejected by the Jews, but accepted by the Gentiles.

Quite right, they were broken off for their unbelief, but you stand by your faith. Do not be conceited, but fear... (Romans 11).

I permitted myself to be sought by those who did not ask for Me; I permitted Myself to be found by those who did not seek me. Therefore, thus says the Lord God, "Behold, My servants shall eat, but you shall be hungry. Behold, My servants shall drink, but you shall be thirsty. Behold, My servants shall rejoice, but you shall be put to shame. Behold, My servants shall shout joyfully with a glad heart, but you shall cry out with a heavy heart, and you shall wail with a broken spirit. And you will leave your name for a curse to my chosen ones, and the Lord God will slay you. But my servants will be called by another name." (Isaiah 65:1,13-15)—Christians! Jesus was rejected by the Jews, but accepted by the Gentiles.

Then Miriam and Aaron spoke against Moses because of the Cushite woman whom he had married, for he had married a Cushite woman... (Numbers 12:1). Moses married a Cushite—a black African woman.

Then Jesus entered a house, and again a crowd gathered, so that he and his disciples were not even able to eat. When his family heard about this, they went to take charge of him, for they said, He is out of his mind (Mark 3:20-21). Moses was criticised by his family because he took a Gentile wife. Jewish people criticise Jesus because, in figure or in type, He took a mainly Gentile wife: the church. That is what the book of Ruth is about—a Jewish man took a Gentile wife and a baby was born who was called 'the redeemer' in Bethlehem.

Then Moses returned to the Lord, and said, "This people has committed a great sin, and they have made a god of gold for themselves. But now, if Thou wilt, forgive their sin; and if not, please blot me out from Thy book which Thou hast written!" (Exodus 32:31-32). Moses prayed to God to forgive the sins of his people and Moses was willing to bear the consequences of their sin and their guilt.

But Jesus was saying, "Father, forgive them for they do not know what they are doing" (Luke 23:34).

For you have been called to this purpose, since Christ also suffered for you, leaving you an example for you to follow in His steps, who committed no sin, nor was any deceit found in His mouth; and while being reviled, He did not revile in return; while suffering, He uttered no threats, but kept entrusting Himself to Him who judges righteously; and He Himself bore our sins in His body on the cross, that we might die to sin and live to righteousness; for by His wounds we were healed (1 Peter 2:21-24).

Jesus prayed to God to forgive the sins of His people and He was willing to receive the consequences of their sin and their guilt.

So he was there with the Lord forty days and forty nights; he did not eat bread or drink water. And he wrote on the tablets the words of the covenant the Ten Commandments (Exodus 34:28). Moses fasted for forty days and forty nights to bring a covenant to God's people.

And after he had fasted forty days and forty nights, He then became hungry (Matthew 4:2). Jesus fasted for forty days and forty nights to bring a covenant to God's people.

Since then no prophet has risen in Israel like Moses, whom the Lord knew face to face (Deuteronomy 34:10). Moses had a face to face relationship with God.

No man has seen God at any time; the only begotten God, who is in the bosom of the Father, He has explained Him (John 1:18). Jesus had a face to face relationship with God.

Whenever Moses came out and spoke... the sons of Israel would see the face of Moses, that the skin of Moses face shone. So Moses would replace the veil over his face until he went in to speak with Him (Exodus 34:34,35). When Moses met

God face to face, he glowed supernaturally.

And He was transfigured before them; and His face shone like the sun, and, His garments became as white as light (Matthew 17:2). Jesus glowed supernaturally like Moses.

In Exodus we read that God spoke to Moses directly from heaven and a voice was heard.

And Jesus answered them, saying, "The hour has come for the Son of Man to be glorified." "Father, glorify Thy name." There came therefore a voice out of heaven: "I have both glorified it, and will glorify it again" (John 12:23,28). God spoke to Jesus directly from heaven.

In the epistle of Jude, verse 9, we read that an angel guarded the tomb of Moses.

And behold, a severe earthquake had occurred, for an angel of the Lord descended from heaven and came and rolled away the stone and sat upon it.

And his appearance was like lightning, and his garment as white as snow; and the guards shook for fear of him, and became like dead men. The angel answered and said to the women, "Do not be afraid; for I know that you are looking for Jesus who has been crucified. He is not here, for He has risen..." (Matthew 28:2-6). An angel guarded Jesus' tomb.

Then Moses said to God, "Behold, I am going to the sons of Israel, and I shall say to them, 'The God of your fathers has sent me to you.' Now they may say to me, 'What is His name?' What shall I say to them?" And God said to Moses, "I AM WHO I AM". And He said, "Thus you shall say to the sons of Israel, I AM has sent me to you" (Exodus 3:13-14). Moses revealed God's name to God's people.

"I manifested Thy name to the men whom Thou gavest me out of the world; Thine they were, and Thou gavest them to Me, and they have kept Thy word. And I am no more in the world; and yet they themselves are in the world, and I come to Thee. Holy Father, keep them in Thy name, the name which Thou hast given me, that they may be one even as we are... While I was with them, I was keeping them in Thy name which Thou hast given Me..." (John 17:6,11). Jesus revealed God's name to God's people.

When the layer of dew evaporated, behold, on the surface of the wilderness there was a fine flake-like thing, as frost on the ground. When the sons of Israel saw it, they said to one another, "What is it?" For they did not know what it was. And Moses said to them, "It is the bread which the Lord has given you to eat" (Exodus 16:14-15). Moses fed God's people in large numbers, supernaturally.

And ordering the multitudes to recline on the grass, He took the five loaves and the two fish, and looking up towards heaven, He blessed the food, and breaking the loaves He gave them to the disciples, and the disciples gave to the multitude, and they all ate and were satisfied (Matthew 14:19-20). Jesus fed God's people in large numbers, supernaturally.

Since then no Prophet has risen in Israel like Moses, whom the Lord knew face to face, for all the signs and wonders which the Lord sent him to perform in the land of Egypt against Pharaoh, all his servants, and all his land, and for all the mighty power and for all the great terror which Moses performed in the sight of all Israel (Deuteronomy 34:10-12).

Moses did miracles, signs and wonders as no other had ever done.

But the witness which I have is greater than that of John; for the works which the Father has given Me to accomplish, the very works that I do, bear witness of Me, that the Father has sent Me (John 5:36).

The Lord Jesus did works, did signs and wonders, did miracles, as no one else has ever done.

Then he took the book of the covenant and he read it in the hearing of the people; and they said, "All that the Lord has spoken we will do, and we will be obedient!" So Moses took the blood and sprinkled it on the people, and said, "Behold the blood of the covenant, which the Lord has made with you in accordance with all these words" (Exodus 24:7-8).

Moses went to a mountain, made a covenant with blood and covered God's people with that blood.

And while they were eating Jesus took some bread, and after a blessing,

He broke it and gave it to the disciples and said, "Take eat; this is my body." And, when He had taken a cup and given thanks, He gave it to them, saying, "Drink from it, all of you; for this is My blood of the covenant, which is poured out for many for forgiveness of sins" (Matthew 26:26-28).

But when Christ appeared as a high priest of the good things to come, He entered through the greater; and more perfect tabernacle, not made with hands, that is to say, not of this creation; and not through the blood of goats and calves but through His own blood, He entered the holy place, once for all, having obtained eternal redemption (Hebrews 9:11-15).

The Lord Jesus went to a mountain, made a covenant with blood and covered His people with that blood.

There were many great men of God in the Old Testament—Elijah, Isaiah, Jeremiah, Samuel, David—just to name a few. But there was only one prophet like unto Moses, the Lord Jesus Christ, the true Messiah of Israel.